COME HOME FOR

CHRISTMAS

COME HOME FOR
CHRISTMAS

JESUS IS CALLING YOU
BACK TO THE GREATEST
STORY EVER TOLD

MATTHEW WEST

with Matt Litton

W Publishing Group

An Imprint of Thomas Nelson

To Emily, Lulu, and Delaney
Coming home for Christmas will always
mean coming home to you.
—MW

Come home, come home, come home,
Come home for Christmas.
Let your heart return once again
To the joy and the peace,
The love and the hope.
It's all right here waiting
For you to come home for Christmas.

CONTENTS

One

AN INVITATION HOME

The Good News of Christmas

THERE IS WINTER . . . AND THEN THERE IS WINTER in the Midwest. I am talking about the bitter cold, snow, ice, and strong winds that cut through any coat, hat, scarf, or gloves. The kind of winter that takes your breath away when you walk out the front door, gets right into your bones, and makes your teeth chatter. Many of you know exactly what I am talking about. Growing up in the Chicago suburbs, I got used to winter temperatures like the one on Christmas Eve in 1983 that notched a glacial negative twenty-five degrees! It makes the cold where I live now in Tennessee seem trivial. I remember as a kid how many

1

of my friends would travel somewhere warm with their families after school got out for the holidays to escape the cold. But not my family. My dad was a preacher, and most years, when we had a few days around Christmas to get away from Dad's church responsibilities, we headed some three hundred miles north of Downers Grove, Illinois, to a not-so-tropical paradise called Mason City, Iowa. If you look at a map, you'll find Mason City is almost as far north as you can go in Iowa and not be in Minnesota. For Dad, that trip meant coming home for Christmas.

My dad grew up in Mason City, and most of my cousins still lived there. It was a Christmastime tradition for us to make the trek for just a day or two for a family Christmas visit to Grandma's house. When I close my eyes, I can still picture the long interstate drive, speeding past piles of new snow and sitting in the backseat next to my brothers in my parents' old red Ford station wagon. I remember how we would listen to Christmas music the whole drive, and I can still hear my favorite classic, "I'll Be Home for Christmas," playing on the radio as we'd pull up to the modest home that belonged to my grandma, Luella West. There wasn't enough room for all of us to stay comfortably, but somehow, we would always manage to squeeze in for a visit. It was important to her that everyone was invited home for Christmas. And no matter what Mom and Dad had going on during the Christmas season, we always said yes to her invitation to visit.

Now, my grandma had raised ten kids—nine boys (including my dad, Joe) and one girl. She was a tiny lady, not even five feet tall, but she was strong, loving, and a fierce protector of the refrigerator door in her kitchen, making sure it stayed closed. My dad tells some great stories of just how destitute they were when he was growing up. My grandpa worked at the local meatpacking plant while Grandma took care of all the kids. Before they had running water in the house, they were only able to fill one bathtub with warm water. So, my dad and his siblings would draw straws for bath time because none of them wanted to be among the last to get in that water. Dad says sometimes you could actually get out of the bath dirtier than when you went in! Grandpa struggled with alcohol until Grandma West hit him with a frying pan. Somehow in that exchange he found the Lord, and they never missed another Sunday at their local Assemblies of God church, but that is probably a story for another book.

All of her children grew up and had kids of their own, which meant Grandma had a small village of grandchildren to buy presents for and a lot to do in order to host all the families that she insisted visit at Christmas. My dad's brother Jim was killed in Vietnam, so there was always an empty chair at the table at Christmas. Even with the joy of so many grandkids, I think that was a painful part of the holidays for Grandma West and the rest of the family. It didn't stop her from saying yes to Christmas, though. I

COME HOME FOR CHRISTMAS

was pretty young when my grandpa passed away in 1984. But the invitations to her home kept coming, and so did her thoughtful Christmas gifts to her many grandchildren. Every single Christmas of my childhood, I could always count on finding the same blunt object, perfectly wrapped, that jingled when I shook it, left under the tree from Grandma to me (more on that in the book's final chapter).

The Iowa holiday gatherings weren't perfect—sometimes they were chaotic and stressful—but each visit was something we all treasured. Now that I am much older and can look back on those days with some perspective, I realize that it was my grandma West's sacrifice that made those Christmas visits feel special. You know, I still love classic Christmas music, and I can't hear "I'll Be Home for Christmas" without thinking of the way my dad faithfully made the pilgrimage home each year for the holidays—and how Grandma would make everyone feel like they belonged.

Christmas Is a Homecoming

I've always loved the way Christmas felt like an invitation home—from my family home as a kid, to visits to Grandma West's, to driving home from college in my Honda Prelude, and to the moment I get home to Nashville and to my girls for Christmas. A few years ago, as I was singing at the annual lighting of the Christmas tree in the town square of Franklin, Tennessee, I was struck by the magic of that special moment. This little town south of Nashville does Christmas right. Old-time Christmas movies are playing at the local theater. Folks are dressed up like they stepped out of a Charles Dickens novel. A children's choir is practicing their big number, all while the mayor prepares to lead the entire town in a countdown to the lighting of the tree in the town square. It's about as festive as festive can get!

Seeing all this gave me the idea to invite people from around the country to take part in a hometown Christmas celebration. I sat down and wrote a Christmas song one evening at my Story House studio, which brought back memories of my favorite Christmas songs on the radio and those snowy drives to my grandmother's house in Iowa each year. The song also evoked the special moments I experienced in Christmas services at my dad's church on Hobson Road and how I feel when I finally get home from that very last tour of the season and walk into my house to celebrate Christmas with the people I love. The song was a personal reminder that in the middle of whatever is happening in the world, and whatever is happening in my life, Christmas is a time to return to the wonder, hope, joy, love, and peace offered to us when we turn our focus to the gift of Jesus. "Come Home for Christmas" was born as a song and a yearly event to invite people to celebrate

COME HOME FOR CHRISTMAS

the true meaning of Christmas. Every year, hundreds of people make the journey to Tennessee, and we celebrate Christmas together!

The theme of that song still speaks into my life in many ways as I prepare my heart for Christmas each season. I have been moved by how God has used the message of coming home. Christmas is a time when we are all invited to physically come home to family. It is a season when we are called to let go of past grievances, make amends, forgive, and allow God to mend relationships that may have become broken over the years. Christmas is an invitation to embrace compassion and offer our presence and our resources to people in need. Christmas is the time to celebrate and share the good news of the gospel with the world. God took the song and the event and did something I didn't expect in my life and in the lives of the people around me. "Come Home to Christmas" was more than a classic Christmas tune and gathering—it started a movement of people making the journey back to the heart of why we celebrate the season. It became a reminder that no matter how far we wander from home, we are always welcome back into the arms of Jesus. Christmas has always been a call back to our true home.

You see, Christmas is the story of God inviting us back to Him. God loved us so much that He sent His only Son—the Wonderful Counselor, the Prince of Peace, the Everlasting Father—helpless into a manger so He could grow up, walk in our shoes, and finally go to a cross to die for our sins. Christmas celebrates the person of Jesus, who is our invitation to come home to the Father. That first Christmas in Bethlehem began with a heavenly celebration that invited us all with "good news that will cause great joy for all the people" announced by angels (Luke 2:10). Christmas means coming home to the good news that God has stopped at nothing to find us and bring us back to Him. And that is something worth hanging lights, decorating trees, and baking cookies for—laughing, singing, giving, loving, and celebrating.

Who Is Invited to Christmas?

I love Christmas so much that my family has given me the nickname Mr. Christmas. And you better believe that Mr. Christmas loves throwing Christmas parties and having Christmas get-togethers (especially my Come Home for Christmas events). This time of year, there always seems to be a guest list for holiday events. A friend of mine works at a corporation that has their Christmas party at a hockey game each December—but you have to be on the guest list to get into the suite. In the capital of the music world in Nashville, there are always swanky holiday parties hosted by big record labels, and you have to be on the guest list to get in the door. Even the fundraisers at Christmastime usually require an invitation to get in! One of the things I remember fondly about visiting my grandma when I was young was that we always knew we had an open invitation to her place (as long as we kept the refrigerator door closed). And one of the special things about the real story of Christmas is that there is no VIP list limiting who can and can't come home for Christmas.

The Bible tells us in John 3:16 that God sent His Son to save the world. Not just a carefully selected list of who's who. Nope. The world—meaning the whole world—is invited to respond to His invitation. The "John 3:16ness" of God means that there is a pretty long guest list for His Christmas party. What does that look like? Throughout His teaching, Jesus used stories called parables to show people how the kingdom of God works. In the Gospel of Matthew, Jesus described a wedding banquet where invitees decided not to show up. He said that the host of the party told his servants to go find people who would say yes to the invitation: "'Go to the street corners and invite to the banquet anyone you find.' So the servants went out into the streets and gathered all the people they could find, the bad as well as the good, and the wedding hall was filled with guests" (22:9–11).

In Luke 14, while Jesus was having dinner at the house of an important religious leader, He told another curious story about invitations that we call the parable of the great banquet. He said:

A certain man was preparing a great banquet and invited many guests. At the time of the banquet he sent his servant to tell those who had been invited, "Come, for everything is now ready." But they all alike began to make excuses. The first said, "I have just bought a field, and I must go and see it. Please excuse me." Another said, "I have just bought five yoke of oxen, and I'm on my way to try them out. Please excuse me." Still another said, "I just got married, so I can't come." The servant came back and reported this to his master. (vv. 16–21)

Again, Jesus was telling the story of a party or feast where those who were invited decided not to show up.

In the first century, if someone was throwing a party—just like today—they would send out invitations for an RSVP. When the meal was ready, the host would send a servant to bring the guests to dinner. In that culture, it would be considered insulting not to show up. Of course, think about all the preparation you go through to have a party. How would it feel for the people you invited to back out at the last minute? The food is made, the table is set, the drinks are poured . . . and the guests decide to ghost you? In Luke's parable, the guests have RSVPd but decide other things are more important than showing up. Instead of canceling, the host decides the party will go on! Jesus explained what the master chose to do with the feast: "Then the master told his servant, 'Go out to the roads and country lanes and compel them to come in, so that my house will be full. I tell you, not one of those who were invited will get a taste of my banquet'" (vv. 23–24).

Both stories reflect the truth that the kingdom of God is going to look a lot different than people think. But another reason these parables are so powerful is that Jesus was pointing out how important it is to respond to His invitation. In both parables, servants were sent out to collect everyone around town who would say yes. In Matthew's account, anyone who would say yes was welcomed in (the good and the bad). In Luke's retelling, the poor, the lame, and the sick (all the people who wouldn't have been high on dinner invitation lists) got invited. The only consistent thing about the people who made it to the feast was that they all said yes to the invitation.

When I read these stories, it makes me think about how God is always inviting me closer to Him. I think the way we celebrate Christmas reflects what we believe about the kingdom of God. We often miss the point that Christmas is the invitation to come home to Jesus. I hope I wouldn't be one of those people in the parable too busy to show up to the party, but honestly, how often do I get so preoccupied with what I am doing that I miss the invitation from God to join in what He is doing?

How often do you get too busy, too distracted, too focused on the wrong things, and miss the point of Christmas? Maybe these stories Jesus tells highlight how easily we can lose sight of the reason for the season. But the parables should also remind us of God's grace in offering us an invitation to His lavish banquet, regardless of what we have done, where we have been, or how long we have been gone. As I think about the invitation to come home for Christmas, I wonder how I am responding to God's RSVP this season. How are you answering God's invitation to come home to Him this Christmas? What if Christmas begins when we say yes to His story for us?

Christmas Means Saying Yes to the Party

When we look at the biblical account of Jesus' birth, it is so interesting that all the important characters involved in the story said yes to an invitation to participate in God's plan for the first Christmas. Have you ever thought about how Mary had to say yes to the angel Gabriel's question of whether she would consent to being the mother of God's only Son? To be honest, I had never noticed this until recently, when I was studying the Gospel of Luke. When Gabriel told Mary of all that was about to unfold in her life, she responded, "I am the Lord's servant. . . . May your word to me be fulfilled" (Luke 1:38). She wasn't an unwilling participant in God's plan to redeem the world. She actually RSVPd for the party that would unfold in Bethlehem.

And it wasn't just Mary who said yes to God's invitation. Joseph had to agree to take Mary as his wife *after* she had been found to be with child. Can you imagine the gossip those two dealt with in their small town as the news unfolded? In Israel at the time, Mary could've faced some pretty harsh consequences for being an unwed mother, and they would have been tough to endure as a young teenager. The Gospel of Matthew tells us that Joseph considered quietly divorcing Mary until an angel showed up in a dream and told him what was up: "Do not be afraid to take Mary home as your wife, because what is conceived in her is from the Holy Spirit" (1:20). Joseph followed through with his yes to God's command: "When Joseph woke up, he did what the angel of the Lord had commanded him and took Mary home as his wife" (v. 24). I love how Joseph was a man of action—he literally just rolled out of bed and followed God's directions.

Even the three wise men's adventure to seek out the Messiah at the end of a mysterious star was a profound act of saying yes. They had to plan a long journey from the east and carry some carefully curated presents with them. They even went to King Herod, who had a scary reputation, looking for the newborn King! Going to Herod to ask about a newborn king may not have been the safest move. They must've had some really big faith in what they were going to find at the end of that star. The Gospel of Matthew shows how intent the wise men were on worshiping Jesus as they asked Herod about the star: "Where is the one who has been born king of the Jews? We saw his star when it rose and have come to worship him" (2:2).

And we even see a yes from the shepherds as they received an angelic invitation in the middle of the night to join in the first Christmas party. They immediately decided to clock out and leave their jobs (and flocks of sheep) behind to go stumbling through the dark and into that small town of Bethlehem, searching for this baby in a manger: "When the angels had left them and gone into heaven, the shepherds said to one another, 'Let's go to Bethlehem and see this thing that has happened, which the Lord has told us about'" (Luke 2:15).

While Christmas is the story of God inviting us home to Him in the person of Jesus, it is also a story of how Jesus entered into this moment through the faith-filled yesses of people like you and me. You see, even the story of that first Christmas was built on the people who said yes to God's invitation. But we also have to slow down.

Recognizing God's Invitation

I vividly remember those Christmas mornings as a kid and how my brothers and I always scoped out the gifts with our respective names on them. In fact, we'd quickly map out which gift we wanted to open first as soon as we caught our breath from running downstairs. I usually found which package looked like it might hold the pair of Air Jordans I had been holding out hope for all year. The Christmas morning madness was just about to begin, and we would soon be swimming in a sea of crumpled wrapping paper and presents. And just as our hands touched that first present, we would hear, "Hold up, boys!" Dad's voice always brought the room to a standstill.

We would turn to see him holding up his Bible, and we three brothers would let out a collective groan of disappointment. Don't get me wrong; I love the Good Book, but it was the timing I took issue with on Christmas mornings! As a kid, it felt like some cruel form of punishment, a parent's ultimate power move to remind their kid who's really in charge! And every year, we would stop and read from Luke 2. Each year it was a different family member's turn to read the story of the birth of Jesus. My youngest brother's turn was the most painful when he was learning how to read, and time stretched on for an eternity as he struggled to pronounce words like *swaddling* and *manger*. After the reading, Dad would lead us in prayer, and his "amen" was the checkered flag that set us free to open gifts.

Of course, Dad wasn't trying to annoy us—there was a method to his madness. By opening the Bible, he was inviting us home to the truth of Christmas. The gifts waiting under the tree were never the point of Christmas—the day was about the immensely greater gift of Jesus. My dad wanted to make sure we never let a Christmas pass without missing God's invitation.

Now that I'm a dad, you better believe I enjoy driving my own children crazy on Christmas morning by holding up my Bible and stopping to read from Luke 2. Of all the Christmas traditions our family carries on, this is my favorite. For a sacred moment, the chaos and excitement of Christmas morning comes to a brief standstill. We quiet our hearts, we still our spirits, and we recognize that God is calling us home to the greatest story ever told, the greatest gift ever given, and the greatest love the world has ever known.

A Standing Invitation to Come Home

The good news of the gospel is that we all have an open invitation to come home for Christmas. But why do we miss it? Why do we so often ignore God's invitation home? You know, I first started dreaming of the Come Home for Christmas message in 2020 when I was off the road because of the Covid pandemic. My newsfeed seemed to be full of bad news, chaos, and despair. I remember how the idea felt like an invitation to return to the joy, peace, love, and hope of that special night in Bethlehem and something we all desperately needed—to return physically and spiritually to Christmas. At the risk of sounding cliché, I know for certain that God wants to bring you home this Christmas.

I don't know exactly what that means in your life today as you read these words. Maybe it simply means getting in a car and driving three hours to be with family. Maybe, if you're being honest, Christmas just hasn't felt the way it used to. Maybe you feel so overwhelmed by the things on your to-do list that you've tended to miss the heart of Christmas in the past. Maybe you have made some decisions in your life that have separated you from a close relationship with God. I'm confident He wants to bring Christmas to your heart this season with boundless healing and redemption. The truth about Christmas isn't complicated. On that holy night in Bethlehem, God was writing your name on an invitation to eternal life—one that still stands today. Jesus is just waiting for you to say yes.

And when I think back on Christmases as a kid, I realize that I learned much more about the heart of Christmas from my visits to Grandma West's house than I ever could have realized. Coming home is more than a feeling, more than an obligation. It isn't perfect and isn't without grief, but coming home is saying yes to love, yes to sacrifice, yes to joy, and yes to the Savior. I learned that no matter where you are and what you have been through, you are always welcome home for Christmas. You see, before Christmas is anything else, it is the story of a God who has crossed the universe to come to you. He loves you so much that He was born into a manger, died on a cross, and was resurrected so you can come home to Him.

Maybe this is the Christmas you can say yes to His invitation home to joy. I hope this is the season you say yes to the wonder of a child. Maybe this is the year you accept His invitation home to healing and forgiveness. I believe God is waiting for you to say yes to peace and compassion. This Christmas season I want you to come home to the manger and to a story that is still true. I hope you'll take a break from the busyness of this time of year, waiting expectantly to hear God's invitation in a new way. This is the "why" of this book you hold in your hands. Don't let the holiday season come and go without the story of Jesus' birth transforming your life. I pray that you will come home to the heart of Christmas in a whole new way and say yes to the Savior who came down from heaven just for you! I hope your journey through this book will open your heart to return to Him once again and embrace the greatest gift you could ever receive: "Today in the town of David a Savior has been born to you" (Luke 2:11).

COME HOME QUESTIONS

* What is your fondest Christmas memory as a child? What was special about it?

* What busyness do you need to put aside this season in order to recognize God's invitation home?

* What are the things in your life keeping you from the heart of Christmas?

* Who do you need to reconcile with or forgive this Christmas?

* Which of the characters in the nativity story most resembles where you are in your journey with God this Christmas season?

* What invitation is God asking you to say yes to right now?

Two

COME HOME TO WONDER

Wide Awake on Christmas Eve

I CAN CLOSE MY EYES AND SEE IT. THE VIEW through the frosted window of my bedroom in that tiny childhood home on Janes Avenue those mornings after the first snowfall. The once-brown lawns and unkempt winter driveways were suddenly hidden by sparkling white powder, making everything look brand-new. The rooftops, mailboxes, and trees were beautifully blanketed as the sun reflected off the bright, clean sheets of ground, calling me and my brothers to make our mark with snow angels, sleds, snowmen, and, of course, snowball fights. That first arrival of Midwestern winter always brought with it the anticipation that Christmas wasn't too far away. And that meant the annual tradition of driving from our suburban home into the big city of Chicago for a family evening of Christmas shopping and sightseeing.

The festive storefront decorations and twinkling lights along the Magnificent Mile are a breathtaking sight for anyone of any age. As our family walked the city sidewalks together, I probably looked as wide-eyed as Buddy the Elf when he arrives in the Big Apple for the first time. The busyness of holiday shoppers up and down the street, the great big Christmas tree all lit up in Grant Park, the "Santa's helpers" in every store, the toys on display in storefronts, and snowflakes floating softly down around us from between the towering skyscrapers were sensory overload for me and my brothers, inducing that special kind of Christmastime excitement that would keep us wide awake at night (and drive Mom and Dad nuts).

I remember the feeling of that first sight of the piles of gifts left for us underneath the tree as we rushed downstairs way too early on Christmas morning. I can recall the joy in our parents' eyes through each moment of our yearly Christmas traditions and the peace that came with knowing I was deeply loved. Christmas was also a time of service for our family as Dad pastored his church through the busy season of celebrating Jesus' birth. And I always looked forward to our Christmas Eve service.

I loved how the flames of those small white candles flickered through the darkened sanctuary, casting our shadows across pews with the congregation singing "Joy to the World" during the candlelight service. I can remember watching with fascination as the flame was passed from person to person, and the song's refrain resonated through the warm sanctuary: "And *wonders* of His love, and *wonders* of His love, and *wonders, wonders* of His love." You know, sometimes during the Christmas season that warmth of nostalgia comes flooding back to me, and I can find myself singing quietly as I go about my holiday routines. "And wonders of His love . . ." Christmas can awaken a powerful sense of wonder in our hearts.

This holiday season I want to invite you to wonder a little bit about wonder. I know the word *wonder* can mean something different depending on your outlook, but I think we all can identify it as a familiar sensation. And if we are honest, we have a longing for it. You see, wonder can be the feeling of awe that makes you pause for a second in the midst of life's busyness, take a deep breath, and look around just to take it all in. Wonder can be the intrigue of the question: *How did they do that?* Yes, wonder can be the stuff of shooting stars, July firework shows, or the sight of snow-capped mountains stretching a mile high. The look in the eyes of little children as we sing Christmas carols and that giant tree in the town square of my hometown, Franklin,

Tennessee, explodes into white lights for the first time each December? That's wonder.

But I believe these daily hints of wonder are echoes of something deeper and more eternal. You see, real wonder springs up from a burning bush in the middle of a wilderness, or a man struck blind and knocked from his horse on the road to Damascus. Just imagine the wonder of finding an empty tomb and the stone rolled away. Yes, wonder is the first cry of an infant being born on a cold winter night in Bethlehem. Wonder is innocent, childlike, and full of the amazement of life's power. Wonder is the steal-your-breath-away impact that a miracle makes when it crashes into our lives. Wonder is in the sense of love we feel when we know we have arrived at our true home. It is as unexplainable as it is real. Yet, as quickly as we can be struck by wonder, it can just as quickly seem to disappear from our lives. Yes, even in the season we should experience it the most, we can fall out of wonder.

From Wonder to Wondering

We all know that the wonder created by Santa Claus, Elves on Shelves, and reindeer with red glowing noses fades with the passing of our childhood. We lose the wonder that kept us wide awake on Christmas Eve. We lose wonder in the things that we know are trivial in the grand scheme of life. But as we grow older, we still have a deep longing for real wonder—a hunger for wonder that is deeply spiritual. For the kind of eternal wonder that makes us run to God with the open hands and hearts of a beloved child asking, "What's next, Father?"

We allow the eternal wonder of life to slip away from us. Even the worship-filled wonder of God's great love story is overshadowed by a different type of wonder. I'm sure you can relate to the anxiety-filled uncertainty of a kind of "wonder" that comes at us each day in a world that can't stay focused on what is true and eternal. The wonder and anticipation of life gives way to "wondering" what is next. That eternal type of wonder is hijacked by the brokenness of a world full of sin and chaos, giving way to

"I *wonder* what the results of my biopsy will be."

"I *wonder* how I am going to pay the mortgage this month."

"I *wonder* if my marriage is going to make it."

"I *wonder* if I'll have a job after next week's report."

"I *wonder* if my kid will ever come back to church."

"I *wonder* if the economy will recover."

"I *wonder* if there will be a war."

"I *wonder* if God still loves me."

"I *wonder* if I can be forgiven."

We learn to live with the doubtful side of wonder that the Enemy uses to make our stories feel divorced from the greatest love story ever told. Yes, I actually think there is an Enemy who wants us to grow cynical and bitter, to close off our hearts from the truths of God's miraculous love . . . to lose our way home. But I believe God is calling each of us to return to that sense of wonder that is deeper and more lasting than the most excited and sleepless Christmas Eves of our childhood! What if we could return to seeing Christmas through the eyes of the children we once were? What if we could come home to see the story of Jesus' birth in a new light, being blown away and born again by the miracle of the greatest gift ever given?

You Are Not Alone in Your Wondering

If you have lost the wonder of Christmas, you are not alone. If you find yourself consumed with the wrong kind of wonder, let me assure you that there was certainly much of the same kind of "wondering" in the times leading up to that first Christmas. The world back then was just as full of uncertainty, anxiety, and pain as it is today.

Luke 2 begins, "In those days Caesar Augustus issued a decree that a census should be taken of the entire Roman world." The world Jesus was born into was no safe or peaceful place. The story of the world's first Christmas is set with the nation of Israel captive under the tyranny of Roman occupation. The Romans were the greatest army in the world and had conquered Israel. Herod the Great, a prominent character in Luke's account of Jesus' birth, was a ruthless leader put into power by the Romans. He had built a huge military base for the Roman soldiers right outside the walls of the temple in Jerusalem, the religious center of Jewish life, just to make sure everyone knew who was in charge. So, as the nativity story begins, life was tough for God's people, and they were longing for the kind of Savior they hoped could help throw the Romans out.

Mary and Joseph had their own set of worries and anxieties as they traveled for the mandatory census that had been ordered by the emperor of Rome. First of all, they had to consider if anyone in their hometown would believe them when they announced Mary's pregnancy and the visit from the angel of God. Can you imagine the heavy "I wonder" questions weighing on Joseph's mind? *I wonder what people will say when Mary tries to explain to them that she is carrying God's Son. I wonder how I am supposed to raise the Son of God.* And what must Mary have been wondering about? *I wonder why God would choose me. I wonder if I can go through with this.* And then, of course, there was the challenge of making travel plans for the family. How would Joseph find a safe and comfortable place for his pregnant wife to rest when they finally arrived in Bethlehem?

I imagine the uncertainty that may have consumed the other characters in the story of the first Christmas. What about the three wise men who had traveled so many miles to meet with that ruthless King Herod? They wondered if they had made a mistake by going to King Herod with news of that curious star and a child being born. God had to warn them in a dream that Herod was out to get them. They knew they were being hunted and had to wonder if they could make it back to their own country safely. Or what about the shepherds tending to their flocks at night? They easily could have been worrying about the same kinds of things that occupy our minds from day to day. Maybe they were wondering if they could make their donkey payment, or if their sick parent would be okay, or maybe they were worried about layoffs in the shepherding industry. The more you read about what was happening in the historical setting around the time of the nativity, the more it becomes clear that the characters in the Bible's account of Jesus' birth had every reason to be consumed with the *wrong side* of wonder. If you are consumed with more wondering than wonder this Christmas, I'd say you are just like the main characters of the nativity story. Of course, God had a plan for all our worry, anxiety, and wondering. He was about to introduce the wonder of His love into human history.

What If Your Heavenly Father Desires Wonder for You?

When I think of the "wonder of His love" lying in that manger on the first Christmas, I am reminded that it begins with understanding the heart of our heavenly Father and the truth that God really does see me as one of His children! I have a friend who preaches that the good news of the gospel of Jesus begins and ends with the words summarized in John 3:16. He says that is all the theology necessary to share the love of God with the world. You may know that verse by heart: "God so loved the world that he gave his one and only Son, that whoever believes in him shall not perish but have eternal life." These words from the Bible are packed full of wonder. They hold the meaning of Jesus' birth. It is the theme of God's plan for you that began in a manger in the small country town of Bethlehem. We tend to lose the important theme of our story because we forget the absolute wonder of God's love for us. The Christmas story is the very beginning of the bigger truth that God loves you no matter where you've been or what you've done or where you are right now. You are one of God's children.

God Invites You Back to the Wonder of Children

Consider the lengths we go to as parents to bring wonder alive for our kids—especially during the Christmas season. As a dad, I've worked really hard to pass on the little traditions of West family Christmas for my girls in the way my mom and dad did for us. All because I want them to taste that sense of wonder I experienced as a kid. When they were young, we would bake cookies and pour a glass of milk to leave out for Santa on Christmas Eve. Once the girls went to sleep, I made sure to eat the cookies carefully, leaving only a few crumbs just to see the amazement in their eyes the next morning. One year, I even left bits of carrots and some oats strewn along the sidewalk so my girls could see where Santa's reindeer had been eating while they waited outside for Santa to deliver our presents. I'll never forget the wonder I saw in their eyes as they discovered that Santa and his reindeer really did stop by for a visit.

I also remember dressing up in a Santa costume to make an appearance on Christmas Eve for my daughters, nieces, and nephews when they were all really little. One of those years I said goodbye after taking pictures with the kids and told them my sleigh was parked just down the road. I walked out the front door, and I actually started running down the street while the kids watched and waved until I was out of sight. You can imagine that running in a Santa suit in some heavy boots with a pillow stuffed in my shirt probably looked ridiculous to the neighbors. I was completely out of breath and sweaty when I snuck back in the house through the back door to find out what the kids thought about their visit from ol' Saint Nick. I still wonder how many kids have grown up in our neighborhood sharing stories about how they saw Santa Claus jogging on Christmas Eve!

I know I am not alone in the crazy things I would do to make Christmastime special for my kids. So many parents go to great (and hilarious) lengths each year to find unique hiding spots for their kid's elf. My friend and his wife have contests to put the elves in the most ridiculous places throughout the house after the kids go to bed each night. During peak Elf on the Shelf rage, I remember social media accounts posting the funniest elf pictures and poses. Another friend of mine took the Santa game to the next level. He even bought a pair of oversized boots so he could track mud and leaves into his living room to make "Santa's footprints" around the kids' presents. I bet you have some of your own great stories too. You get the picture. We love our kids so much that we will go to great lengths to bring wonder to their lives.

And that love is the real source of wonder. There is something about childlike wonder that goes deeper than just the silly things we do to make memories for our children. In case you doubt the power of childlike wonder, let me remind you of a verse where Jesus was teaching the disciples about what it truly meant to follow Him: "Unless you change and become like little children, you will never enter the kingdom of heaven" (Matthew 18:3). I think becoming like children means that we release our anxiety, hurts, and cynicism into our heavenly Father's hands so we can embrace how much we are truly loved. Try to think about the kind of love we have for our own children when you consider God's love. If we take the love we have for our kids and multiply it a thousand times over, it doesn't even come close to how much God loves each of us. Our heavenly Father launched an invasion of love that changed the history of the world to help us find our way back home to His loving arms.

Step into a Story of Eternal Wonder

We only need to open the Bible to hear the voice of God's love calling us home. Into a world of anxiety and uncertainty, God brought wonder. The real Christmas story is one of coming home to a wonder like the world has never seen. You see, Christmas is the tipping point, the catalyst, the invasion—that stable in Bethlehem is the very birthplace of wonder.

Just look at how *wonder* is written throughout the story of Jesus' birth.

The three wise scholars discovered that uncharted and

unexplainable star and had studied prophecies of a new king being born. They packed up their things, said their good-byes, and set out on a journey spanning hundreds of miles into a foreign country to search for evidence of a prophecy fulfilled. They were like the Indiana Jones characters of the Christmas story, setting out with their maps and tools in their search for the Messiah. I imagine the excitement of their journey was way bigger than walking the Magnificent Mile with my parents in Chicago! And how did they know to choose their gifts of gold, frankincense, and myrrh that would symbolize the kingship, divinity, and sacrifice of a Savior? They were on that kind of great adventure. To finally be captured by the *wonder* that the great star led not to a Roman-appointed king or a palace or a religious temple or even a capital city, but to a tiny little village in the middle of nowhere and a baby in a lowly manger.

In the dead of night, a group of manual laborers worked faithfully to watch over their flocks of sheep. Maybe they had just finished a lunch break there on the night shift. Maybe they were playing games or giving silly names to the sheep, because I can't imagine shepherding is a terribly exciting gig. Under the silence of the clear night sky, with the sheep bleating softly in the pasture—it happened: suddenly, these men were stunned by the shock and awe of an angel of God appearing to tell them, "Do not be afraid" (Luke 2:10). (That first moment of seeing an angel had to be scary because that is *always* the first thing angels say to humans in the Bible.) Just as they were catching their breath, steadying themselves, with their heart rates returning to normal, imagine how they felt at the sight of a host of angels filling the night sky, singing praises, and proclaiming the birth of Jesus! It was a celestial choir belting out a heavenly anthem. "Suddenly, the angel was joined by a vast host of others—the armies of heaven—praising God and saying, 'Glory to God in highest heaven, and peace on earth to those with whom God is pleased'" (vv. 13–14 NLT). Can you imagine the *wonder* of hearing the first Christmas carol sung by a "vast host" of angels?

I'm sure every mother reading this can identify with how Mary felt on that first Christmas evening. She was going through the uncertainty and miracle of childbirth with the one added expectation that the angel Gabriel had told her she was giving birth to the Messiah! I doubt there has ever been a more anticipated Christmas gift. Mary had to be consumed with wonder as she took her first look into the eyes of baby Jesus that night. Can you imagine the things she must've felt in those first moments of Jesus' life as she wrapped Him in blankets to keep Him warm? Mary's prayer of thanksgiving and praise when she heard Jesus was coming, "My soul glorifies the Lord and my spirit rejoices in God my Savior, for he has been mindful of the humble state of his servant" (Luke 1:46–48), is full of *wonder*.

Of course, as a dad who is always concerned about looking out for my family, I think about the relief Joseph

COME HOME TO WONDER

must have felt after that long journey to Bethlehem. Finding no room in the inn, he had finally landed a safe place for his pregnant wife in a stable. And what about the faith he had in the message from the angel, the belief of Mary, and her willingness to carry this child? How did Joseph feel in those first moments of Jesus' entrance into the world? Was he amazed to see the visiting shepherds and wise men bow down to worship baby Jesus? Sometimes I think the faith Mary and Joseph showed in God and in each other is one of the most beautiful parts of the nativity story. That kind of faith is a *wonder* to behold.

"And Wonders of His Love"

The nativity story calls us home to that *everlasting* wonder. So, whenever I hear "and wonders of His love," it reminds me that Christmas is the time when we are called to lean into the wonder of the God who loved us so much that He sent this baby Savior wrapped up in the warmth of a manger, adored by his mother and father, announced by a host of angels, visited by shepherds and wise men. I am reminded that the wonder of Christmas is that God "moved into the neighborhood," as Eugene Peterson says in *The Message* version of the Bible (John 1:14). He moved in to be close to us.

As we enter the Christmas season, we marvel at the

reality that God broke into time and space and history and our very lives with the birth of Jesus. We try to imagine the peace and quiet awe of those moments after the birth of Jesus with songs like "Silent Night." We read of Mary's song of praise and the visitors who arrived to worship this baby. But the truth of God's love story is that this birth was not only a beautiful beginning. Jesus' arrival served to end the reign of sin and death forever.

We sit before this peaceful scene, understanding that the God of the universe was setting in motion a holy sacrifice to bring us into His love forever. With Jesus' first cries, wonder broke into creation. As a baby took His first breaths, wrapped safely in His mother's arms and under the protective watch of His father, all the powers of darkness began to shake with fear. Because at this very moment in Bethlehem, the God of the universe was calling you and me home to His infinite and inescapable love. What a wonder to know that we worship the God who loved us enough to send His Son to the manger, to the cross, and to the empty tomb just to invite us into eternal life.

This Christmas, if we can truly embrace that kind of eternal wonder, there can no longer be room for worry or anxiety. Coming back to the birth of Jesus helps us shake off all our other "wonders" of life. I believe wonder is often the distance between what we can understand and God's extravagant, unfathomable love breaking into our lives. Because our God is Immanuel—God with us—embracing wonder means approaching every day with the faith that looks to God with anticipation and asks, "What's next, Father?"

When I think about coming home to wonder, I am thankful that growing up, I knew my parents loved me and that no matter where I went or what I did, they were always going to love me. I would always be welcomed home. My deep love for my own children is the reason I want to share wonder with them. Our heavenly Father's deep love for us is the reason wonder was born in that tiny town of Bethlehem. I hope you will recognize all the ways He is calling you back home to that wonder in your own life.

Christmas invites us to experience an eternal kind of wonder, the kind you can't grow out of. So, you can come home this Christmas to the heart of the Father, where you will never have to wonder if you are worthy of love again. This Christmas invitation is to let your breath be taken away by the "wonders of His love"—to consider the true meaning of wonder entering the world.

COME HOME QUESTIONS

+ Can you remember the wonders of the Christmas season as a child? What were they?

+ If you are a parent, how do you create wonder in the lives of your own children? How much more do you think God wants to draw you into the wonders of His love this season?

+ Do you have a list of wonderings that are keeping you from the wonder of Christmas this season? What's on it?

+ How does the story of the wonders of the nativity point you back to God's extravagant love for you?

+ How can you share the wonders of God's love with others this season?

Three

COME HOME TO JOY

The Secret of Live Nativity Scenes

WHEN I WAS TEN YEARS OLD, MY FAMILY DECIDED to save up our money throughout the year so we could travel to Disney World for our Christmas celebration. As a kid, I was convinced that Disney was, as they say, the "happiest place on earth." I was so excited about it that I didn't sleep for days leading up to our trip. The anticipation was incredible as we piled into the car and headed out of that suburban, snowy Chicago winter for the warm climate of central Florida. But none of the advertisements or daydreams I had about hanging with the world's most famous mouse on our Christmas vacation could have prepared me for what it was actually like to walk through the ticket gates into a not-so-magic kingdom experience.

You may have guessed already that there are some unforgiving realities about spending Christmas at Disney World. Maybe you've seen it firsthand. It is the most chaotic, hectic, and crowded experience you can possibly imagine. The lines for everything, from buying popcorn to going to the bathroom to getting into rides like Peter Pan's Flight, were a mile long and moved about as quickly as the animatronic characters on the cool, dark shores of Pirates of the Caribbean (you know, the ones bolted to the ground). I think the stressful experience even caught my dad off guard. Dad was always an expert vacation planner, but nothing about our trip to Disney went according to plan. And the people who crowded in around us at the park were generally impatient, surprisingly sweaty for December, and not the least bit shy about stepping over you to get a place in line. Thinking back on it now, I imagine their vacation plans were not working out for them either.

I went into Magic Kingdom wearing my brand-new T-shirt—it was a Snoopy shirt that read "Stay Cool" (no one could really stay cool in the unusually hot weather that afternoon). I was minding my own business, resting on a railing, when a crowd of tourists with cameras and backpacks sped by me like a herd of buffalo and accidentally pushed me over the railing. They sent me falling backward into a huge muddy puddle! I spent the rest of the day covered in dirt with scrapes and bruises, and to add insult to injury, my new Snoopy shirt was ruined. I was so mad, the "Stay Cool" message on my shirt took on a whole new level of irony. I was just too young to know what *irony* meant. My family managed to laugh our way through the experience, and eventually, I even started to smile about the irony of my sweaty, mud-stained T-shirt right along with them. Needless to say, the adjectives we use to describe Christmas—peaceful, calm, merry, *joyful*—were nowhere to be found inside that park. In fact, the experience was so unmagical that my family voted we should stay home for every Christmas from then on.

Honestly, the best part of going to Disney was leaving and making the journey back home for Christmas together. We took a family vote and decided to pack up early, pile back into Mom and Dad's old red Ford station wagon, and head home. All the promises and advertisements of the places and things that would bring me joy ended up being empty. And yet I noticed that as a family, we continued to choose joy. It was a great life lesson for me. We never had much money growing up and stayed on a tight budget when we traveled. But I have fond memories of how Dad would make so much of the trip a game for us. For example, when we would stop at a fast-food restaurant, the challenge was to see if all of us could eat for under five dollars. (Now remember, this was the 1980s.) It was a great strategy by Dad because we would actually get excited about trying to eat cheap!

On the drive back from Disney, we stopped at a burger joint, and I kept badgering my dad to hand me the ketchup bottle. I was being obnoxious and impatient with him to the point of annoyance. Dad had been driving all day, so he responded to my behavior by calmly finishing putting ketchup on his burger, looking me right in the eyes, aiming, and squirting that ketchup all over my face! It was so out of character for my dad to do something like that, and I sat there stunned with ketchup running down my cheek. Within a few seconds, the entire family burst into laughter until we were all in tears. Our family made so many fun memories in those moments on our way home—the joy of that experience had *nothing to do* with the circumstances around the trip we had planned. I learned that joy isn't about where you go or how you get there. Joy is about the direction in which your heart is pointed. I guess coming home for Christmas has always brought me back to the joy of the season.

When Joy Feels Like Coming Home

We talked about the importance of wonder breaking into the world that very first Christmas. Why? Wonder is the effect that joy makes in the world—it is an invitation to turn your heart in the right direction. We throw the word *joy* around all the time, but I think we need to take a moment to think about what it means when we sing about it in Christmas carols or even when we read about it in Scripture. We use *joy* for so many different things— "Opening that present brought me joy," "The Cubs winning the World Series brought me joy," or "Getting that raise brought me joy." But the "joy" of getting a new iPhone can't be the same joy we find in the Bible. That kind of joy is just a shallow emotion attached to a conditional situation that passes quickly, right? That's not the "joy, joy, joy, joy, down in my heart" that kids sing about at Vacation Bible School. So, when we talk about joy during the Christmas season, when we light the candle of joy during Advent services, when we sing about it, what *exactly* are we talking about?

One of my favorite Christian authors, C. S. Lewis, wrote a famous book called *Surprised by Joy*, where he described a little about joy, saying that it "must be sharply distinguished both from Happiness and from Pleasure. . . . I doubt whether anyone who has tasted it would ever, if both were in his power, exchange it for all the pleasures in the world."[1] Wow. That's exactly why he is one of my favorite writers! So, joy is something more substantial than happiness. And when you have it, you wouldn't trade it for anything.

I read recently that the word *joy* is referenced more than four hundred times in the Bible.[2] I also did a little Bible study and looked up how the word is used when we find it in the New Testament. The Greek word for *joy* is *chara*, and it's defined as gladness, cheerfulness, or, my favorite, *calm delight*. Bible scholars agree with C. S. Lewis that joy reflects a steadiness and depth not associated with a passing event. True joy isn't dependent on our circumstances, which also means this joy the Bible speaks of isn't something that can be taken away. We may not always feel it in the moment or recognize it, but it is still there.

Joy takes center stage as we celebrate Advent in our faith communities. A lot of churches these days use Advent candles to mark the weeks leading up to Christmas. In the third week of the Advent celebration, there is a pink candle known as the "shepherd candle." This candle is meant to represent the joy that comes through Jesus' birth and the salvation He offers us. This third week of celebration focuses on Philippians 4:4–5, where the apostle Paul told his readers, "Rejoice in the Lord always. I will say it again: Rejoice! Let your gentleness be evident to all. The Lord is near." Paul said joy is found in the truth that God is near us! Christmas is the story of God coming near us. So, it is Jesus' birth that brings deep and lasting joy to the world. And when we focus our hearts on Him, that joy tends to spread like the flames of a candlelight Christmas service.

Just like with most of the spiritual truths of Christmas, we have to trade in all the trivial, the consumerist, and the worldly ideas about joy to embrace its eternal truth. We

COME HOME TO JOY

have to let go of pop-culture ideas about joy to get to that inner, immovable definition of the joy that only God can bring us.

Another thing we can probably all agree on about joy is that it seems to be kind of a rare commodity in today's world. Think about how often you really find people who seem to be burning with joy. How many times do you miss it in church service—a place where joy should be breaking out everywhere? When was the last time you could say that you really were aware of joy in your own life? Or when was the last time you brought joy to someone else? The angel brought "good news of great joy" (Luke 2:10 ESV), but when was the last time you really experienced that for yourself?

The reality for so many people is that Christmas is anything but a time of joy. So many things compete for our attention during this season—office parties, church functions, neighborhood parties, or even the stress of Christmas shopping can fill our calendars to the point of exhaustion. For some people, Christmas is just a season of too many conflicts and uncomfortable family get-togethers with weird uncles and strange family dynamics. There are so many obligations that can make us feel stretched thin emotionally, relationally, and even financially. It's not like we need any more added noise out there in the world, but the hustle and bustle and material focus of the season can definitely work to darken our joy light if we have any burning at all. Remember, there is an Enemy who is intentionally working to steal our joy. He thieves by using discouragement, grief, and the temptation to believe that all hope is lost. But God has given us a story of joy unlike anything the world has ever seen—if we will just turn the attention of our hearts toward the first Christmas.

The Story of Jesus Is a Story of Joy!

The story in Bethlehem begins with an announcement that joy has *arrived*. We talked about the *wonder* of the angel of the Lord suddenly breaking into the night sky and announcing what Jesus' birth would mean to the world. *Joy* is what the angel promised those terrified shepherds: "But the angel said to them, 'Do not be afraid. I bring you good news that will cause great joy for all the people. Today in the town of David a Savior has been born to you; he is the Messiah, the Lord. This will be a sign to you: You will find a baby wrapped in cloths and lying in a manger'" (Luke 2:10–12). It wasn't just joy that the angel promised; it was a *great* joy for *all the people* because of baby Jesus. What a way for Jesus to make an entrance! And I love that the angel explained this joy was for "*all* the people." That means the big announcement wasn't just for a certain group that looks or talks or acts a certain way or has reached some elite level of social status. No—the announcement was for *all* the people, even you and me! That is some really good news.

44

So this angelic message sent the shepherds into town look-ing for the baby Jesus. In other words—they had to turn their feet and their hearts toward the promise of great joy.

The shepherds had to take a little bit of a road trip home to find Jesus. I don't know for sure how far outside of Bethlehem they were when the angel appeared to them, but they immediately clocked out of work to search for the brand-new baby in town. Because the angel told them they would find Jesus in a manger, they knew to look in the parts of homes where the animals were kept. Bible scholars say that Mary and Joseph were probably staying with a distant relative, and since a manger was a feeding trough for live-stock, they were housed with animals and were pretty low on the guest list of relatives. I can imagine how this group of shepherds went peering into the backyards of homes, look-ing under fences and over walls for the promise of great joy. If they arrived in the dead of night, they were probably tripping over each other in the dark until they were able to hear the beautiful cries of the newborn baby ringing out from down the street.

I wonder what the journey to find Jesus was like for the foreign scholars following the curious star. I've read Bible scholars who say that it is unlikely that the shepherds and the wise men showed up at the same time to find the baby lying in a manger, which is a little disappointing because of how much I love seeing those extravagant live nativity scenes that churches put on at Christmastime with the animals and the shepherds and wise men all hanging out together in the cold. They have a drive-through live nativity at a church in Nashville with goats, horses, cows, donkeys, and people dressed as Mary, Joseph, shepherds, wise men, and angels—all crowding around baby Jesus. Whether the animals and all these characters being present is historically accurate or not, the reenactment of that scene teaches us all we need to know about the source of eternal joy!

You see, it doesn't matter what route they had to take to arrive at the manger—stumbling through the dark or following a star. It doesn't matter whether they were rich, poor, short, tall, fat, skinny, brilliant, dull, manual laborers, or royalty. It doesn't matter what stress, anxiety, grief, depression, or illness they brought to the manger. What matters is that they all bowed before the baby and worshiped Him. It is that adoration and worship of Jesus as the Messiah that is the true source of joy. The focus of those live nativity scenes points us to the truth about joy as we witness the characters turning their hearts toward Jesus, the deliverer of joy. The first Christmas exploded joy into the world, and as Jesus grew up and began His ministry, joy was a theme of His teaching.

In fact, Jesus boldly promised that joy comes from Him. Twice in the Gospel of John, Jesus told us that we will find joy in His love: "I have told you this so that my joy may be in you and that your joy may be complete" (John 15:11). Jesus invites us to follow Him into a restored relationship with God, which completes our joy and makes it untouchable to the world. What about all the terrible circumstances and grief that life throws our way? Don't worry, because just a chapter later, Jesus explains, "You will grieve, but your grief will turn to joy" (16:20). Remember that the angel prophesied "good news that will cause great joy for all the people" (Luke 2:10). Do you want to experience great joy this Christmas? You only need to turn your heart in the direction of the same good news that shepherds and wise men found in a Bethlehem manger. Our joy originates in the gift of God's only Son. That's right, that means God is in the *joy* business!

God's Joy Is Beyond Circumstances

I have one friend who is facing the first Christmas since his wife passed away this year. I have another who will walk through her first Christmas as a single mom. I know yet another family who will spend this Christmas season in a hospital as their child continues cancer treatments. It levels me when I think of the grief, stress, and anxiety present in the lives of so many people I love during the holiday season. But my faith is lifted beyond measure to see that the very people who are facing these hardest of times are also steadied by a joy with roots so deep it seems unshakable. They teach me so much about eternal joy. They show me the way to joy by the truth that they have focused their hearts on Jesus. And they live with a joy so luminous it seems to jump from their hearts to mine when I spend time with them. It isn't the happy-go-lucky, aw-shucks kind of thing; it is as certain and as strong as steel because it has looked in the face of life's hardest moments and has seen Jesus there too.

The people glowing with inner joy even through tears this Christmas challenge me to understand that we are talking about a quality that transcends even our toughest circumstances. We can all allow the messes in our lives to overshadow the message of God's love and faithfulness from time to time. We can focus on our fear, anxiety, and negativity instead of the love, peace, and hope we have in Jesus' birth. We can believe the stories, lies, and hollow messages the world is ready and willing to offer us every minute of the day. But when we look toward the light that is the love of Jesus, something amazing happens.

Eternal Joy Is Contagious and Uncontainable

I traveled not long ago to perform at a prison in Michigan. We stood in the middle of a basketball court on a make-shift stage in an environment where you'd never expect to find joy. I was absolutely floored by the inmates, who were singing praise songs along with us and laughing at my jokes. Their joy was a light that made us forget about the walls and chain-link fences, the watchtowers, and the security guards all around us. That situation made the Bible's words seem a little different when I read them: "Consider it pure joy, my brothers and sisters, whenever you face trials of many kinds, because you know that the testing of your faith produces perseverance" (James 1:2–3). As I watched the prisoners' joyful worship, I was reminded how supernatural life can be when we turn our hearts toward Jesus in praise and adoration. I walked away understanding how deep that reservoir of inner joy runs in the hearts of those who believe in Him. Real joy can't be kept out or shut in—even by prison walls.

I've taken trips with Operation Christmas Child to tiny, remote villages in Panama and to Colombia to deliver shoeboxes filled with toys, school supplies, and personal hygiene items. During one of these trips, I sat with the children as they opened boxes filled with soccer balls, stuffed animals, and essentials like toothbrushes, pencils, and socks. We were in one of the most desolate villages I had ever visited, and I was taken aback by the joy that burned bright in the midst of extreme poverty. Honestly, the joy I have witnessed over and over when I take part in mission work and meet people with such deep faith is overwhelming. It always brings my focus back to the truth about Christmas. We should never be surprised when God takes our hands and leads us somewhere—even to remote villages in faraway countries. Real joy transcends languages and borders.

One of the formative experiences of my adult life arrived in the most unexpected and unfortunate circumstances. When the pandemic hit in 2020 and shut down the music industry, I canceled tours, postponed events, and found myself like everyone else: feeling anxious, uncertain, and lost. That's when I picked up my old Gibson guitar in the Story House studio and began to worship over social media platforms with whoever wanted to tune in. I started a weekly "Quarantine Quiet Time" and held some virtual events and concerts. Those moments sparked a season of growth when I started my podcast and dreamed about a way to celebrate "Come Home for Christmas" each year. As I turned my heart away from the depressing news cycle and the discouraging cancellations and focused on Jesus, it led me back to the great truth about eternal joy. By joining others in worship, I was able to break out of a spiral of discouragement. Real joy shows up no matter how dark the world may seem.

I am also reminded of a sweet lady named Debbie who flew from California with her husband to be part of the annual Come Home for Christmas event I host in Nashville every December. Through tears, she told me that the day before their flight, she received the news that she had been diagnosed with cancer. She said, "I'm not starting chemo yet, so we decided to make the trip to see you anyway!" We prayed together and had an incredible weekend celebrating Christmas with three hundred other people from around the country. There was such a deep joy evident in her presence. She was effervescent, and it had nothing to do with her circumstances. Real joy can even break through a diagnosis.

You see, we find joy when we look to its source. And when we come home to joy, we become carriers of joy to each other as we move through the world with our hearts pointed toward Jesus. Our unshakable joy can point others to the source of great joy. As one of my pastor friends always says, joy kind of spreads like the flu—it can be passed from person to person. These people, these places, these expressions of great joy continue to challenge me to keep my heart focused on the Christ child. Real joy springs up whenever and wherever we turn our hearts toward Jesus.

Joy Is Calling You Home

The other day, my mom reminded me of a gift I gave her during the first Christmas when I came home from college. It was a wooden sign that read "Home for the Holidays," and on the back, I wrote this note to her: "No matter how far away I go, I'll always come home for Christmas." My mom shared with me how much joy that brought her, and she still has that sign all these years later. When I think of joy, I always think it begins when we turn our hearts and our lives toward that place of belonging.

At the end of every year, when the tour bus drives back to Nashville after I've played my last Christmas concert, I experience this fundamental truth about joy. As I sit here writing, I can hear the familiar sounds of arriving home after unloading. The squeaking garage door as it opens for me to pull in. The click and last quiet growl as the engine of my car shuts off. I can feel the turning of the key, opening the door to my house, and taking that first step on those old hardwood floors to see the dogs running down the hallway, barking frantically like they haven't seen me in a year. I breathe in the sweet scent of my daughter Delaney's sugar cookies baking in the oven. And, of course, I love the sound of my wife, Emily, announcing to the whole house, "Daddy's home! Christmas can begin!" The hugs and kisses from Emily and my daughters as they walk into the kitchen to greet me. Even the sound of my bags hitting the floor and the sensation of setting down all the stress and busyness of the outside world. It is Christmas, and I am home—I am finally where I belong. All is well; it is a deep sense of calmness and delight! I am home with my family who truly loves and delights in me, and I in them.

Here is one thing I am certain of about the story of Christmas: that sensation of calmness and delight comes when you turn your heart to the miracle of God's love. I love the description of joy as "calm delight." Like the old carol "Silent Night" says, "all is calm." And the truth is that we experience the calm delight of joy because of how much our heavenly Father actually delights in us! If we could talk to the shepherds and the wise men who stood before that baby Savior on the first Christmas, I bet they would tell us that arriving at the manger felt like coming home. Why? Because I believe as they worshiped Him, they knew they were right where they belonged.

Sometimes I think it is easy to feel like the little boy in the Christmas movie *The Polar Express* who continually echoes the refrain, "Christmas just doesn't work out for me." In some seasons of our lives, we can feel downtrodden and separated from joy. I know some days during the busy holiday season, joy can feel distant, but returning to joy is simple. We only need to follow the example set before us in those first moments of the Christmas story as a weary group of travelers knelt to worship and adore the baby Savior asleep on the hay. If you are missing joy this season, I want to remind you that you are being invited home by a God who loves you and delights in you. And as we turn our hearts toward Him, our lives can be full of the truth of the words penned by Henry van Dyke in 1907: "Joyful, joyful, we adore you, God of glory, Lord of love."

These beautiful lines remind us that no matter where we go or where we've been this year, we are invited to come home to joy, to where we belong, to the place where our hearts turn in adoration and worship of the Savior who delights in us. Even if this Christmas season finds you sick, grieving, or just having a tough time, joy isn't off-limits to you. In fact, maybe right now, as you read these words, is the very moment to allow the joy of Jesus to be your strength. Joy was born for all creation in that little manger in the remote village of Bethlehem. And joy is there for us when we, just as the shepherds and wise men did, fix our gaze on Immanuel, "God with us."

COME HOME QUESTIONS

+ How would you describe joy in your life? Are you experiencing joy this Christmas season?

+ What is the difference between the way the world talks about joy and the eternal joy written about in the Bible?

+ How often do you focus on praise and adoration of Jesus in the same way the wise men and shepherds did? How can that help you return to joy?

+ What circumstances are keeping you from joy? Do you really believe that God delights in you and is calling you into joy?

+ How can you share joy with others during this season?

Four

COME HOME TO HEALING

Christmas Is the Season of Waiting

I'M ONE OF THOSE PEOPLE. YOU KNOW THE KIND. THE kind who likes to put their Christmas decorations up long before the rest of the neighborhood. If it were up to me, I'd start putting up the tree the day after Halloween like they do at Walmart and Lowes these days. My wife requires that I allow just enough time for her fall decorations to have their moment to shine. But you'd better believe that the very minute that last bite of Thanksgiving turkey is eaten in the West house, I'm headed straight for the attic to break out the many storage crates and boxes of Christmas decorations. That time of decorating for Christmas with the family kicks off my favorite few weeks of anticipating Christmas Day.

Of course, one of the major headaches that comes with putting up the Christmas stuff is the yearly process of sifting through broken things. I have become convinced there is a bear living in our attic who waits for us to pack all our decorations away, and then he stomps all over everything. Because there are always decorations, ornaments, and strings of lights that somehow don't survive their year in storage. No matter how carefully Emily and I pack away the Christmas stuff each January, we always open boxes of ornaments to find a handful chipped, broken, or cracked from their journey to the attic and back again. The worst part is sorting through the strings of lights. No matter how you pack them up, they always get tangled, and it only takes one tiny bad bulb for an entire string to go dark. I don't have a lot of patience with the process of finding out which strings of lights still work and which don't (picture Clark Griswold throwing a temper tantrum in the front yard as he kicks a plastic Santa). The point is that each Christmas season begins with the little reminder that things wear down, age, and eventually break.

The Reason for the Season

Honestly, broken things are a recurring issue as Christmas draws nearer on the calendar. When the girls were young, Christmas Eve was always a time that would find me stressing to put together toys, dollhouses, and bicycles (and doing it without breaking them in the process). As much as I want to be, I am usually not the "fix it" kind of guy when something breaks. You might say I come from a long line of soft hands. My dad, the Reverend Joe West, always joked during a failed attempt to fix something around our house that his hands "were apparently made to carry a Bible, not a hammer." I guess I grew up knowing my genetic disposition when it comes to fixing stuff. My wife, Emily, will be the first to tell you that if I try to repair something like a broken toilet, I will likely make matters even worse. But that doesn't mean I don't try. I will never forget the Christmas one of my daughters came to me holding her favorite gift from Christmas morning that was now broken, and asking, "Daddy, can you fix it?" As a guy who can't fix anything, I was going to try to do whatever I could to help her.

The Christmas season brings a flood of nostalgia and emotion and has a way of churning up stuff that has been hidden in the attics of our lives for the past year—just like those broken ornaments and lights. The celebrations and festivities of Christmas exist alongside the reality of brokenness. As we set the table for Christmas dinner, we come face-to-face with the memory of loved ones who will not be with us this year. As we work on fixing strings of lights, we cannot hide from the lights that have gone out in our own lives. With the countdown toward Christmas set in motion, things like depression, chronic illness, job loss, or strained relationships become more evident. While there are wonderful things about Christmas, the great reality is that broken hearts, broken bodies, broken humanity, and broken creation are the true "reason for the season."

Even the pop-culture Christmas stories we love reflect our implicit need for healing—the truth that there is something in all of us that yearns to be fixed. Because all great stories begin with some great inner struggle: Buddy the Elf sets out to "fix" the absence of his real father in his life. Rudolph the Red-Nosed Reindeer is looking for confidence and acceptance. In Charles Dickens's famous story *A Christmas Carol*, the greedy businessman, Ebenezer Scrooge, is deeply bitter and lonely. And, of course, in my all-time favorite Christmas movie, *It's a Wonderful Life*, George Bailey is afflicted with something the movie calls "worse than sickness"—his heart is plagued by a deep discouragement. All these stories begin in a place of brokenness. And maybe that is where Christmas should truly begin. Whether it is out in the open for everyone to see or hidden in the attics of our hearts, we can take this time to acknowledge the brokenness we carry *that we cannot fix on our own.*

When I say I love *It's a Wonderful Life*, I'm not exaggerating. I watch it multiple times every Christmas season. There is a scene where the main character, George Bailey, runs up the stairs to check on his daughter, who has fallen sick. She has a flower her teacher gave her for Christmas, and as she proudly shows it to her dad, some of the petals fall off. Zuzu begins to cry and asks if her daddy can paste the flower back together. George's love for his youngest daughter comes through clearly in the scene. He pretends to glue the fallen petals back on the flower while sneaking them into his pocket where Zuzu cannot see them. Of course, as I write this, I'm reminded of how it felt when my daughter brought me the new toy she had broken on Christmas morning, looking for help: "Daddy, can you fix it?" We so badly want to fix things for our children. And we so desperately try to fix things for ourselves.

Christmas Is a Season of Waiting

Christmas has to begin with our admission that we are broken and we can't fix what's broken on our own. The reason for the season is found by acknowledging *why* we need Jesus so desperately. God is always focused on healing and restoring what is broken, and that isn't always a quick fix. Before Christmas means anything else, it must mean the commencement of healing for the world. You see, God doesn't really *replace*; He *fixes*. He doesn't magically trade out; He gracefully restores, and that is a process that takes patience and faith. It is important for us to recognize that as we celebrate Christmas each year, we are actively participating in a *season of waiting* for God's healing touch to arrive.

In the days leading up to that beautiful moment in Bethlehem, God's people were waiting and waiting and waiting on God's promise. They had been anticipating the fulfillment of a prophecy from the book of Isaiah for a very long time. And remember, the people of Israel were not in a great place during the Roman occupation, so the level of desperation was high. God had made some big promises to His people. Look at what Isaiah had written about that first Christmas and the grand entrance of Jesus into the world: "The Lord himself will give you a sign: The virgin will conceive and give birth to a son, and will call him Immanuel" (Isaiah 7:14).

Isaiah prophesied about the coming of *Immanuel*, which means "God with us." The people were looking for God to arrive among them—to walk with them. But the prophecy didn't stop with the promise of how Jesus would arrive! Isaiah explained further what the coming of the Messiah would mean for everyone: "He was pierced for our transgressions, he was crushed for our iniquities; the punishment that brought us peace was on him, and by his wounds we are healed" (Isaiah 53:5).

Into a world of broken hearts, broken bodies, broken humanity, and broken creation, Isaiah promised that the first Christmas would introduce true and lasting healing into the world. And the prophet makes it clear that he was not just talking about physical healing: "He has sent me to bind up the brokenhearted, to proclaim freedom for the captives and release from darkness for the prisoners" (Isaiah 61:1).

Jesus will bring peace, He will heal our wounds, He

will mend broken hearts, and He will release captives from the darkness. Wow. Can you imagine what the people who heard and read and memorized Isaiah's pronouncements thought about the coming Messiah? Imagine what the shepherds were thinking as they knelt at the manger! Remember, Isaiah's words about Jesus were taught to every Jewish child; they were read aloud in synagogue; and they were a big part of the hopes and dreams of the entire nation of Israel. I bet God's people wondered plenty of times if they would ever really come true. I bet there were years of mounting impatience as they suffered under foreign rulers. If they stayed focused on the truth of God's promise, imagine the anticipation. The need for healing of the world was so long overdue. So how long would they have to wait?

Well, it was much longer than the brief four weeks or so between putting the decorations up and the arrival of Christmas Day! The people of God had to wait for the first Christmas for a long, long time.

History teachers and theologians seem to agree that there were a little over seven hundred years between Isaiah's prophecies and the birth of Jesus.[3] That is way longer than many countries in today's world have even been around. Just think about all the stuff you learned in history class about what life was like just one hundred years ago. I don't know about you, but it hurts my head to think of waiting that long for a promise. I get impatient if I have to wait more than five minutes when I'm in line to buy my daughters'

Christmas presents. As a kid, I remember the few short hours I'd let my parents sleep after they put us to bed on Christmas Eve until I woke them up to open presents. It felt like seven hundred years!

That is a long season between the *promise* of healing and the *arrival* of the Healer. And that is a long time to have to hold on to faith in the promise. My point is that if it's true that Christmas is a season of recognizing our need for healing and redemption, it is also true that Christmas calls us to *practice waiting* on the arrival of the Great Physician.

Learning to Wait on God

No one likes waiting. Waiting is hard. And waiting on God is super tough because it requires faith. I think this is why we tend to want to hurry up and just try to replace the things that are broken in our lives. It is hard to wait for God to bring restoration. It doesn't take any faith to replace our spouse rather than fix our marriage. It doesn't take patience to fill our loneliness with an addiction rather than lean on God to help us heal it one day at a time. It doesn't take trust to burn down a broken friendship rather than allow God to restore it. But God wants to fix what's broken, and that requires learning to wait on Him.

When I think about learning to wait on God, I remember several run-ins with health challenges that have threatened my music career. In 2004, I had surgery performed on my arm in a way that left me unable to play the guitar. I had to shut down touring right when I was finally gaining momentum in my career. This led to months of waiting, praying, and trusting God for healing. Just as I was able to play again and seemed to be gaining momentum, I ran into another roadblock. I was so happy to be back on the road that I was performing concerts like an iron man. At one point, I played twenty shows in twenty-one days. And as I was about to make a record called *Something to Say*, I suddenly found myself unable to sing. Ironic, right?

I needed vocal cord surgery to get my voice back. The doctors were very concerned there might be a buildup of scar tissue that could cover the wound, preventing my voice from ever sounding the same again. I had been working for so long to have my music heard, so being told that my voice wouldn't be heard by anyone threw my life into a tailspin. I had to place my faith in surgeons, the power of prayer, and the practice of waiting. Of course, the worst part of that season for a talker like me was to follow the doctor's orders and be still and be silent. I had to be still long enough for the healing to be complete. I had to wait it out. I remember how difficult waiting was through that particular Christmas season until it became clear to me that God was giving me a gift way bigger than getting my voice back. I was learning to wait on Jesus.

I learned that God's desire was not just to heal my body but, even more significantly, to do healing work in my soul. I needed to anticipate the coming of Jesus and be open to what He wanted to heal in me. This season of waiting taught me that coming home to healing means giving up control. Jesus' work always starts with acknowledging that we can't heal ourselves.

You see, we can live with brokenness for so long that it becomes normal and keeps us from our true voice, our true self. Sometimes we can't even see areas of our lives where we need healing until we come before that manger in expectation and waiting. The beautiful thing I experienced while waiting on my physical healing was that I grew so close to the Lord that my perspective on what I was praying for changed. Instead of praying, *Dear God, please hurry up and heal my voice so I can sing*, my heart's posture shifted to, *God, even if You don't choose to heal my voice, I believe You have a better plan, and I will trust either way*. In the waiting, I learned that my greatest need was less about healing and more about a deeper relationship with the Healer.

When Healing Was Born in a Manger

Seven hundred long years of anticipation led to that night of wonder, joy, and the arrival of healing in Bethlehem. The world was no different than it is today, with all its anxiety, unrest, brokenness, and sin. Right in the chaos and desperate need for healing, Mary and Joseph quietly wrapped baby

Jesus and placed Him in the manger. It must have been a scene of peace and serenity like the world had never seen before. As new parents exhausted from their long journey and overwhelmed by the emotions of childbirth, I wonder if they could reflect on what was happening at first. Did they look up to see the great star overhead? Did they hear the angel choir's announcements? Did they actually understand that they were holding the Great Physician in their arms? I wonder if the shepherds who visited that night to kneel before the baby Jesus needed healing. I wonder if they thought of Isaiah's prophecy in those moments.

Whenever I read the nativity story in the Gospel of Luke, I wonder if anyone present could even begin to fully grasp God's plan for this innocent child to break the chains of sin and death forever and "bind up the brokenhearted," as promised in Isaiah 61. All of heaven leaned in with anticipation to watch God's plan unfolding—those little hands reaching out of the manger would grow to become the nail-scarred hands reaching out across all of eternity to you and to me with salvation and healing.

Of course, as Jesus' ministry began, His identity as the Son of God was evident in the miracles of healing He performed everywhere He went. This son of a carpenter wasn't going to spend His life mending broken tables—He was going to mend broken bodies and broken hearts. As He traveled, the Bible tells us that multitudes lined up to be healed by Jesus (Matthew 15:30). Healing would be a major focus of His ministry and a promise delivered, as Matthew 8:17 explains: "This was to fulfill what was spoken through the prophet Isaiah: 'He took up our infirmities and bore our diseases.'"

Jesus gave sight to the blind.

Jesus gave voice to those who couldn't speak.

Jesus gave hearing to those who were deaf.

Jesus gave the power to stand and walk to paralytics.

Jesus healed lepers and all kinds of illnesses.

Jesus cast out demons.

Jesus even raised the dead.

The New Testament references twenty-six specific situations where Jesus performed physical healing. Some asked Him for it, some just touched the hem of His garment, some were brought by friends, and some were simply healed by faith. "Jesus went throughout Galilee, teaching in their synagogues, proclaiming the good news of the kingdom, and healing every disease and sickness among the people" (Matthew 4:23). But Jesus was also busy healing hearts: "When Jesus saw their faith, he said to the paralyzed man, 'Son, your sins are forgiven'" (Mark 2:5). Jesus is a healer of wounded hearts, a healer of broken bodies, a healer of broken dreams. And as we look toward the manger at Christmas and wait on the One who can bring healing to our lives, we can't forget the truth that He has called *us* to participate with Him in the healing of the world.

Sharing the Gift of Healing

Jesus is pretty clear to His disciples about our responsibility to lend a hand to the process of mending the world. The New Testament explains the great challenge Jesus shares with those who choose to follow Him: "When Jesus had called the Twelve together, he gave them power and authority to drive out all demons and to cure diseases, and he sent them out to proclaim the kingdom of God and to heal the sick" (Luke 9:1–2). Jesus invites us to participate in His work of healing! The book of Matthew explains, "Jesus called his twelve disciples to him and gave them authority to drive out impure spirits and to heal every disease and sickness" (10:1). Jesus doesn't just arrive with healing; He passes on healing authority to those who follow Him.

Christmas shouldn't just be a time of waiting on God's healing but also a season when we pass that healing on by sharing God's love with our family, our neighborhood, and the world. If Christmas is truly the turning point where healing entered into creation, how can we turn our perspective toward spreading that good news? Maybe we need to ask ourselves some tough questions this Christmas: *How can I be a person who speaks healing words? How can I be a person who helps heal hearts? How can I better participate in healing the brokenness I see all around me? And how can I share my own miraculous healing and redemption with a world of people who need to see it?*

Whenever I think of how Jesus is calling us to participate in healing, it reminds me of a song I wrote a while back called "The Healing Has Begun." I was inspired by my friend Ginny, who made the choice to terminate an unplanned pregnancy when she was a teenager and carried the shame of her mistake with her for nearly thirty years. She shared with me that after hearing me speak at a conference about how God can bring healing to the broken parts of our stories, she gave that brokenness to God, and that was the first step toward healing. She then took that healing and began to gift it to others. Today, Ginny volunteers to help struggling women who are contemplating the same choice at a crisis pregnancy center in her hometown. She is sharing the healing work of God with others who need it. Ginny's story is a beautiful example of how the Healer continues His healing work through the lives of the ones He heals.

The good news of healing calls us to share the news of our healing with others. Why? Because the birth of Jesus on that first Christmas turned the tide of world history away from brokenness and sin and introduced restoration and healing in Him. We need to shout that from the rooftops this Christmas season, echoing the victorious cry of the old Christmas hymn, "Hark! The Herald Angels Sing," written by Charles Wesley:

> *Light and life to all He brings,*
> *Risen with healing in His wings.*

With the birth of Jesus in that little town of Bethlehem, the redemption of the world was decided, and God is still inviting us to get involved in the inevitable move toward healing. I'm convinced that the bolder we are to share the healing work of God in our lives with the world, the more we bring the healing hands of Jesus to those who need it most. Jesus brings healing into your world and then calls you to carry His healing message into someone else's world this Christmas.

Bring Him What Is Broken

It's probably not going to make the cover of a Hallmark Christmas card, but the truth is that Christmas is actually supposed to be a time when we begin taking inventory of what is broken in our lives. Forget about the broken ornaments, the strings of lights that don't work, the old tree that isn't going to survive another season—it is a time to be honest with God about the brokenness in a family, a time to face up to addiction, a time to address the need for healing in our relationships, in our communities, and in our world. Christmas is when we turn our attention to the truth that the Son of Man didn't come to earth for us to choose to hide in our brokenness but to acknowledge it and place it in the hands of the Healer. As we wait to celebrate the birth of Jesus, we can boldly choose to invite Him into our brokenness. Christmas should be a season when we can be honest with Jesus: "Here is my mess. Here is my wound. I know You are my healer." First Peter 5:10 reminds us, "The God of all grace, who called you to his eternal glory in Christ, after you have suffered a little while, will himself restore you and make you strong, firm and steadfast." God invites you to come home this Christmas before you are healed so you *can* be healed.

Christmas is the season when we come home with the question: *Where do I need healing?* Jesus isn't going to throw out the broken stuff. He fixes the lights. And the baby in the manger that reaches out to you across eternity right now can heal

The relationship that has been severed for years.

The illness that leaves the doctors baffled.

The addiction that won't let go.

The wound from the past that wreaks
havoc on your life still.

The anxious mind.

The weary body.

The troubled soul.

The healing power of Jesus is the very reason the story
of the first Christmas is the greatest story ever told.

Enter the Story of Healing

While popular Christmas stories and movies begin with
some type of brokenness, the thing that really keeps us
reading (or watching) is that they are also stories of healing!
I think we love those redemptive endings because they point
to a powerful and undeniable truth about the meaning of
Christmas. Buddy the Elf finds acceptance with his real
family and learns that he still has value to Santa. Rudolph
finds acceptance from his peers and learns that the red nose
that makes him so different from others is actually a gift to

the world. Ebenezer Scrooge leaves his life of loneliness and greed to become the most generous man in all of England. And then there is George Bailey, who is facing brokenness like many of you may be facing this season in the name of discouragement.

George hides the petals from his daughter Zuzu's "broken" flower in his pocket at the beginning of the movie before he is carried away by an angel to be shown what the world would look like without him. In this alternate reality, the flower petals are no longer in his pocket because his former life no longer exists. After the angel Clarence shows him the reality of what he means to so many other people, George realizes that he has been returned to his true life when he reaches into his pocket and finds the broken petals. I love that this symbol of brokenness signifies the return to his imperfect, beautiful, wonderful life. The movie concludes with the entire community coming home to George's house in a great celebration that reminds me that God doesn't throw anything away—he takes our broken hearts, broken bodies, and broken experiences and uses the material to build beautiful things.

When I think of all the people gathered in that stable and around the manger on the first Christmas night, I have to consider how much brokenness was there standing in the presence of such a promise. I think of what it must've been like to kneel in the presence of the Healer for the first time in the history of the world. And I am humbled by the thought that we stand in His presence today through the power of His sacrifice on the cross. I wonder if this Christmas, before we begin to unpack the boxes of ornaments and lights and sort through what is broken, we would spend some time recognizing that He is waiting on us to bring the broken places in our lives, in our families, and in our world and set them at His feet.

Christmas is a time of returning to the Healer. Jesus' invitation for you to come home to healing is unconditional. You don't need to have everything in order. Christmas calls you to bring your mess into His house and lay it at the feet of the Great Physician. Coming home to healing means that we approach our heavenly Father the same way that Zuzu came to George Bailey with her flower. The same way my daughter brought me her broken toy one Christmas morning. We simply show up with all that is broken in our lives, the areas that need healing and redemption, with open hands and say, "Fix it, Abba." That holy night in Bethlehem, the promised Healer who ultimately chose to break Himself so He could bring wholeness and redemption to our hearts and lives arrived. The birth of Jesus began the countdown to the end of all brokenness, disease, sin, and illness. May we come home to healing, wait in patience and faith, and let the Healer do what only He can do in our lives this Christmas.

COME HOME QUESTIONS

- + What has God healed in your life that you can celebrate this Christmas?

- + Are there some areas of your life you need to hand over to God for healing?

- + Are you holding on to something broken that He wants to fix?

- + How is this Christmas season teaching you to wait on God?

- + What in your life, your family, and your community needs the healing touch of Jesus? Take some time to pray for those requests right now.

Five

COME HOME TO PEACE

'Tis the Season to Hurry, Worry, and Rush Around

CHRISTMAS AND THE PROMISE OF PEACE ARE SUP-posed to be synonymous. You don't have to look far to find references to peace during the holidays. If I am being hon-est, though, one of the themes of my childhood would be "the Chaos of Christmases Past." You see, for the preach-er's family, there is always so much to be done during the Christmas season. Whereas a megachurch might have a multitude of staff to help accomplish things, our church ran on the energy and goodwill of a few volunteers and "free labor," otherwise known as the pastor's family! That was the West family. Christmas meant sidewalks needed to be shoveled, and salt needed to be poured on the icy walkways. It meant the front lawn of the church needed to be decorated and lights hung on the trees. And don't forget the candles for the Christmas Eve service needed to be counted and set out. The annual live nativity? Someone had to clean up after the animals after they, well, you know . . . Yes, every year there was a long to-do list for church services in addition to the usual shopping, cooking, cleaning, wrapping, and preparing for family get-togethers. That always made Christmas a high-stress holiday for the Wests— not that we didn't find ways to make it fun. But I don't know if I ever really thought much about the word *peace* at Christmastime. It was always a season of hurry, worry, and rushing around to get things done.

And yet, the first Christmas began with the hope and promise of peace sung down from the heavens! The shepherds must've had quite a story to tell Mary and Joseph about getting their directions from an angelic choir to find their way to the baby Savior lying in the manger. In the Gospel of Luke, the final refrain of that heavenly serenade is a promise of *peace*: "Glory to God in the highest heaven, and on earth peace to those on whom his favor rests" (2:14). The angels announced that peace had arrived!

Peace is a central promise of the Christmas story. These days, peace is written all over our wrapping paper and holiday cards. I can remember many Christmas sermons preached about peace over the years. And how many Christmas song lyrics mention peace? We sing, "Sleep in heavenly peace," or "His gospel is peace," and of course, "Peace on earth and mercy mild." In the church's celebration of Advent, the second week focuses on peace as a hallmark of Christmas, remembering the angels' proclamation: "Peace on earth." If you just landed here from outer space, I'd bet you would find it pretty ironic that peace is such a huge theme during the holidays. Why does a season that celebrates peace seem so full of chaos?

The Hustle and Bustle of the Season

My friend Bob tells a story of the old days, before online retail was a thing, when he made an early morning odyssey to the local mall to buy his daughter's Christmas present one year. He jumped in the car, queued up a Christmas CD, and pulled into the drive-through at McDonald's for a coffee. The line was twenty cars deep, but that wasn't going to mess with his holiday spirit. He was a man on a mission for Santa Claus. A traffic jam of cars was backed up on the interstate at the mall's exit. Still, he wasn't discouraged. His errand that day? A shipment of the season's hottest new toy (he remembers it as a fairy that flew through the air when you pulled her string) was arriving that morning, and only the first one hundred people in line could buy one.

Bob circled the mall parking lot for thirty minutes to find a place to park. With an hour to spare before the store opened, he parked and jumped out, only to be greeted by the angry yells of a strange man who accused him of stealing *his* parking spot. He shrugged his shoulders and began to jog toward the mall entrance, breaking into a sprint when he noticed the huge line forming outside the toy store. Christmas music floated softly down from the mall's outdoor speakers, and he could barely make out the words "peace on earth" through the restless buzz of slightly impatient but hopeful parents. He anxiously counted the people in front of him. *Ninety-three, ninety-four, ninety-five . . . thank goodness*, he thought. He was ninety-sixth in line! The gate was lifted by a teenage clerk in a Santa's helper outfit, and people began to jockey for position like hockey players in a faceoff. Despite his best Yuletide efforts, he finished as the 101st person in line—just one person too late to get the coveted flying fairy for his daughter.

Bob's hectic holiday adventure is so funny because it exemplifies how often our modern-day Christmas routines are the exact opposite of peace. Christmas just has a way of heightening the hurry, worry, chaos, and crazy! If you aren't fighting the crowds and traffic at the mall, you may get pulled into the drama of family gatherings or find yourself exasperated trying to get the kids to stop fighting long enough for the perfect family Christmas card photo.

There is the stress of choosing the right gift for your boss or the right white elephant present for your coworker's party (you know, tasteful but funny). And what about budgeting the whole holiday to make sure you can pay for it all? Yep, Christmas sure seems to bring all our running, striving, pursuing, buying, and consuming to a fever pitch.

Of course, there are more serious aspects to our talk about the lack of peace at Christmas. Anxiety and depression are already at an all-time high during normal seasons of the year. I read recently that over forty million Americans deal with some form of anxiety.[4] My friend Pastor Brian says that the weeks around the Christmas holiday are the most stressful time of the year for people, but no one really feels like they can talk about it (or preach about it) openly. It's the big secret every pastor knows but can't talk about. He counsels more people with acute anxiety and depression during the month of December than the rest of the year combined! Of course, we have to remember that even in the weeks leading up to Christmas Day, the news cycle doesn't stop churning. That means we are also flooded with doomsday headlines, daily warnings about the next pandemic, the next recession, the next election, the next climate crisis, or the next war that is unfolding. It sure seems like all this talk about peace at Christmas is more of a longing than a reality. It feels like we need peace more than ever. But if peace can't be found in the season that announces its arrival, when can it be found?

A Story of Peace Beyond Circumstances

It is important to remember that, as we consider the promise of peace in our lives and in the world, the setting of the Christmas story was not much different from today. The circumstances surrounding the birth of Jesus were anything but peaceful. Just think about the restlessness in the mind of young Joseph, who got a whole lot more than he bargained for being engaged to Mary. Or what about the worry that may have been in the heart of a teenage girl who had just been told as a virgin she was carrying the Son of God? There was probably some anxiety in Joseph's life as he planned to take Mary, who was in the late stages of pregnancy, safely from Nazareth to his hometown of Bethlehem for the census.

Bible scholars say that the most likely route Mary and Joseph would've traveled from Nazareth to Bethlehem was more than ninety miles long. Most of that distance was across difficult terrain that didn't offer places for them to stay at night. They probably slept out in the elements. I don't know how many of you ladies reading this have been in the late stages of pregnancy, but can you imagine how excruciating it would be to travel that many miles over several days? Remember, they couldn't call an Uber, so the best case for Mary, who was full-term, would've been traveling on the back of a donkey. I imagine that when the two finally arrived at Joseph's hometown, finding a place to unpack, even in a stable around a bunch of animals, had to be quite a relief. Talk about weary travelers! Mary and Joseph's experience leading up to that first Christmas doesn't sound peaceful, does it?

The chaos and political turmoil of that time also rivaled anything we hear on the news today. In the years leading up to that first Christmas, many of the people in Israel were looking for a Messiah to appear who would lead a rebellion to run the oppressive Romans out of their country. And even as the Prince of Peace was being born on that holy night in Bethlehem, King Herod, who had heard of the Messiah's birth from the wise men, was already planning to intercept Him by ordering every baby boy under two years old in the land to be murdered by his soldiers. Joseph and Mary would soon have to run away to Egypt to keep Jesus safe from harm. I guess it is fair to ask the question: Where in this story is the peace that the angels promised?

Jesus Offers More than a Moment of Peace

Peace seems to be in short supply in our world, just like it was hard to find on the first Christmas. Jesus acknowledged a truth about our fallen world when He explained to His disciples: "In this world you will have trouble" (John 16:33). Whenever I hear the phrase "a moment's peace," I think about how the constant turmoil and noise in our world can fool us into believing we're lucky to find a brief feeling of peace in the middle of a chaotic Christmas season. We strive for peace like it's something we can achieve by our own efforts. We are like Ellen Griswold from *Christmas Vacation*, frantically searching for a hidden pack of cigarettes in her kitchen after her relatives have arrived for the holidays. The grandparents are arguing, the teenagers are complaining, and her nerves are already worn to a frazzle. She lights up a cigarette as she listens to her teenage daughter whine about having to share a room with her little brother and utters this stressed-out response: "I don't know what to say, except it's Christmas, and we're all in misery."[5]

You see, we are trained by the world to think we have to go out and make peace, find it somewhere, or take something to get it. The world tells us that peace, like everything else, is transactional. We must earn it, buy it, corner it, find it, capture it with our own efforts. But peace isn't an app on our phones. We can't wait in line for it at the mall, it can't be prescribed by a doctor, and, honestly, we don't even need to sit in a pew to find it. The reality is that all these things are only a distraction. When we give up looking and striving and manipulating and simply turn our attention toward Him, well, peace finds us.

The prophet Isaiah gave several important names to Jesus in his promise of the coming Messiah: "He will be called Wonderful Counselor, Mighty God, Everlasting Father, Prince of Peace" (Isaiah 9:6). Each of His names is a reminder that there is only One who can provide for every single need we have. Are you confused and facing a big decision? His name is Wonderful Counselor. Are you feeling weary? His name is Mighty God. Have you been betrayed and wondered if all love is temporary? His name is Everlasting Father. Is your heart troubled with hurry, worry, and anxiety this Christmas? The Bible is clear that peace is only found *in Him*. Not in a location or a special circumstance—only in the person of Jesus. He is the Prince of Peace today, tomorrow, and forever.

Jesus Is the Prince of Peace

I know I'm probably not supposed to pick favorites when it comes to the names of Jesus. But I just love the name "Prince of Peace." When I say it these days, I feel like I'm exhaling the trouble and anxiety of my life and allowing my heart to be pointed to a humble King who graciously promises the gift of peace, not in some far-off future but right now in this very moment—in this very Christmas season. You know, the song "Hold Me Jesus" by the late Rich Mullins always moves me. In it he sings about shaking like a leaf, prayerfully appealing to God to be his Prince of Peace.

I wonder if you relate to that sentiment like I can. Has the world left you shaking like a leaf this past year? The great beauty of the Christmas story is not found in the circumstances surrounding His birth; it is found in Him, the Savior who has overcome this troubled world!

Christmas celebrates the coming of a Savior who the apostle Paul tells us delivers on His promise of peace: "The peace of God, which transcends all understanding, will guard your hearts and your minds in Christ Jesus" (Philippians 4:7). So the peace Jesus offers is found not in a moment or in a location or in a special circumstance, but in our relationship with Him—in coming home to Him. Despite the stress, anxiety, and worry our world seems to ramp up around the Christmas holidays, the coming of Jesus on that first Christmas was a story aiming us toward the Source of all peace—one that passes all understanding.

The good news of the first Christmas is that directly into the chaos of human history and human experiences, a Prince of Peace was born. God sent His only Son to offer a peace that transcends whatever is happening in your life, in the busyness of this holiday season, and in the greater world all around us. It is a peace that transcends our circumstances. Peace that passes all understanding requires that we open our hearts, take a deep breath, step back, stop what we're doing, and acknowledge who Jesus is and what He can do. That's right—it means we trust Him to provide it. You see, the peace we long for is as simple as leaning on the truth of Psalm 46:10: "Be still, and know that I am God." Embracing peace means letting go of our searching, striving, and achieving and making a spiritual trust-fall into the arms of a Savior.

Peace is the gift we receive when we learn to trust that we are redeemed by His love. Throughout the New Testament, peace is portrayed as a quality we receive in salvation. It is the gift to all who follow Jesus. Jesus offers us *inner* peace. Because of His work on the cross, we have a chance to receive salvation and can rest knowing that God will return to heal this broken world. Jesus brings us into peace with others as He calls us to set aside our differences and serve the kingdom of God to share the good news. As Paul explained in Galatians, "There is neither Jew nor Gentile, neither slave nor free, nor is there male and female, for you are all one in Christ Jesus" (3:28). And when we talk about "heavenly peace," we are talking about *shalom*, the Hebrew word for peace that goes far beyond not fighting with others or peace as we know it. Shalom is how things are meant to be—a peace that is just like heaven—or, as Jesus prayed, "on earth as it is in heaven" (Matthew 6:10).

In the Gospel of John, Jesus left His disciples with an incredible blessing: "Peace I leave with you; my peace I give you. I do not give to you as the world gives. Do not let your hearts be troubled and do not be afraid" (14:27). The reality is that from birth to death to His resurrection—peace was always His desire for us. The Bible is clear that Jesus offers a *heavenly* peace that transcends whatever is happening in your life, in your home, in your community, and in this world around you. That heavenly peace is eternal. So, what is it going to take for you to come home to the peace that Jesus offers this Christmas season?

Coming Home to Peace by Trusting Jesus

What if we really embraced the truth that peace is not something we have to go and find? Peace is not confined to a certain location, vacation, or vocation. I love how the apostle Paul explained, "I have learned the secret of being content in any and every situation, whether well fed or hungry, whether living in plenty or in want. I can do all this through him who gives me strength" (Philippians 4:12–13). The secret of being content is found in trusting in Jesus. It is in Him that peace resides. We will not find peace in the things we buy, in our status, our relationships, or our financial security. We cannot find it in where we go or what we do. We can only find it in Him. That is why it seems to be so rare in today's world—even during the Christmas season.

What if we set down our search for peace and simply learn to be still and trust the Prince of Peace residing in our hearts? The reality is that we can sleep in heavenly peace because our Savior has arrived. We can be still and know that Emmanuel has come. God is with us in this very moment. We don't have to search for an escape from reality in order to find that elusive moment of peace because Jesus stepped into our reality to offer us a peace that will never leave us. We can know peace because our sins are forgiven. We can know peace because death is not something we have to fear anymore. We have peace because we can trust that Jesus walks alongside us. You can be still knowing that Jesus brings peace to you wherever you are—whether that is on your way to the office party, standing in a crazy line at the mall like my friend Bob, working to get your church ready for a Christmas Eve service, or going in for your next cancer treatment. He is waiting for you to be still and trust Him with every territory of your heart.

The peace that passes all understanding is as present in our hearts as it was in the manger that first Christmas. When we take a moment to turn our eyes toward the Source of peace rather than trying to find it on our own, peace finds us. "Be still" in Psalm 46 is a reminder that we don't need to stress, strive, go, do, or perform in order to receive the favor of God. We only need to look toward the manger and open our hearts to Him. And when our hearts come home to peace in Christ, something supernatural happens: we become peace providers for others. Jesus, in His mission statement sermon, said, "Blessed are the peacemakers, for they will be called children of God" (Matthew 5:9). Jesus is calling us to share this peace, this shalom, that He provides for us with the world.

I love the idea that peace on earth begins with God

bringing peace into our hearts. It reminds me of a song that has become part of the hymnals in many denominations: "Let There Be Peace on Earth." I read that Jill Jackson-Miller, who co-wrote the song, actually wrote it while coming out of a terrible time in her life. After attempting suicide, she came face-to-face with God's unconditional love. She explains, "I had an eternal moment of truth, in which I knew I was loved, and I knew I was here for a purpose."[6] Peace that passes all understanding is truly found in the unconditional love of Jesus. Finding that kind of peace is good news that must be shouted from the rooftops, sung in carols, written on cards and across wrapping paper . . . but most of all, it must be shared with our family, our neighborhood, and the world.

Come Home to Peace in Him

Christmas Eve these days is still my favorite part of the holiday because of the break it offers from the hurry, worry, and rushing around of the holiday season. I love the hour when the kids are fast asleep, all is quiet in the house, wrapped gifts are under the tree, *It's a Wonderful Life* is on the television, and I'm sitting by a roaring fire thinking back to how the snow used to fall each Christmas in my suburban Chicago neighborhood as a kid. All is calm, all is bright. It is the seasonal calm before the storm. I know that in just a few hours, the kids will be tearing open their presents, wrapping paper will cover every inch of the floor, relatives will be ringing the doorbell, and Christmas dinner will be prepared. But for those moments, it's quiet, and I'm at rest. On Christmas Eve I always take time to remember our Savior, the Prince of Peace, being born into a manger in Bethlehem. I am intentional about being still and making sure I am placing my trust in the constant Source of peace that passes understanding.

As I think back on those hectic holiday seasons at our family church long ago, I vividly remember how the busyness and chaos gave way to something holy once all the work was done and the Christmas Eve services began. There was something beautiful transpiring as the congregation's voices lifted out of the dark, singing "Sleep in heavenly peace" as snow fell softly outside the stained glass windows of the warm sanctuary. Those memories remind me that we all come together at Christmas with our shared longing for peace—real, lasting, "heavenly" peace. I love the idea that when our search for peace comes up empty, peace finds us. If peace can find us and stay with us, it can be on display in us in the most unlikely places when we cling tightly to the Prince of Peace in our lives.

Have you ever encountered somebody who radiated peace? I've met people who had received devastating medical diagnoses, literally given weeks to live and their lives thrown into a tailspin. Yet, they carried with them a countenance of peace that was palpable. And strong enough to occupy whatever room they were in, even a hospital room. When you see peace on display in an unlikely situation like that, you begin to understand that God's peace can reside in us on the deepest level, unable to be stolen away by the circumstances of our daily lives and chaotic Christmases. I want to experience that kind of peace this Christmas. I want that for you too. Most importantly, God wants that for you.

I don't know where you are this Christmas season, but let me ask: How long has it been since you have slept in heavenly peace? What is it that is stealing your peace? Who or what are the peace thieves in your world? How is the Prince of Peace calling you to be still and trust in Him this Christmas? Maybe it is time to release your restless and anxious heart to Him. What would it look like this Christmas season for you and me to truly come home to the Prince of Peace?

So, what if we accepted that peace on the deepest levels and carried it with us throughout this Christmas season? How can we bring all of the anxiousness—the fears from all the years—lay them at the feet of the Prince of Peace, and dare to believe that His words are true? He promises, "Peace I leave with you; my peace I give you" (John 14:27). As we come home to peace this Christmas, let us look to the One who came to bring peace to our hearts.

COME HOME QUESTIONS

+ What are some of the things that are stealing your peace this Christmas season?

+ In which areas of your life do you need to be still and trust Jesus?

+ How does trust allow space for peace in your life?

+ How can you share the peace that passes all understanding with others this Christmas season?

+ Who can you pray for today who needs the peace of Jesus in their life right now?

Six

COME HOME TO COMPASSION

Showing Others the Way Home

I WANT TO SHARE AN AMAZING CHRISTMAS STORY with you about a little boy named Dax Locke, who sparked a movement of compassion that is still shining in the world today. Dax was born on June 26, 2007, and spent most of his life in hospitals battling leukemia. He and his family lived in a small town in Illinois but had to stay at St. Jude Children's Research Hospital in Memphis, Tennessee, for long stretches of his life. During a final visit, the doctors came into the room and delivered a prognosis to the Locke family that no one ever deserves to hear. The team of medical experts had exhausted all treatment options for Dax's cancer. The doctors believed he probably wouldn't make it to see the New Year. It was devastating news.

Dax's family brought him home from Memphis that September carrying the unimaginable heartache that their little boy might not make it to see his favorite holiday. You see, Dax loved all things Christmas—especially the lights and decorations. I still can't imagine the level of grief they must've been dealing with as they arrived home that fall. One night, Dax's dad couldn't sleep, so he climbed into the attic and brought down every last Christmas decoration. He spent the entire night decorating for Christmas to surprise little Dax when he woke in the morning. The Locke family raised the Christmas tree, hung stockings, and even decorated the lawn. As the family held out hope for one last Christmas with their son, something amazing began to take place around them.

The neighbors on their street quickly learned what was going on and began to decorate their homes and lawns for Christmas. Right there in the seventy-degree weather of early October, when pumpkins and Halloween decorations should've been everywhere, the entire street began to shine at night with Christmas lights. What began with a few neighbors spread to the street and then to the entire neighborhood, showing solidarity with the Locke family. Christmas decorations broke out as quickly as the news of Dax's prognosis was shared until the entire town of Washington, Illinois, was in on the effort. The whole town was completely decked out for Christmas three months early! From the hallways of schools to the light fixtures on streets and even the tree in the town square, the whole community had pitched in to put up lights, hang garland and tinsel, decorate their Christmas trees, and make sure that wherever little Dax went in his hometown—he would find Christmas! To this day, the story of so many people coming together to support and show solidarity with a family experiencing such grief and tragedy still moves me to tears.

As the news spread of the spontaneous outbreak of early Christmas decorations, it began to impact people far from the small Illinois town. For so many people to open their hearts and respond in a way that made Dax's family know they were not alone is one of the most beautiful Christmas stories I have ever witnessed. To me, Dax's story reflects how the kingdom of God works—it points to the truth that we are never alone because Everlasting Love was born that first Christmas. In sharing that love, we show our neighbors that they are never alone. This kind of compassion is what happens when the heart of Jesus is at the center of our celebration.

The most beautiful part of Dax's story is the reality that what began in great tragedy, God continues to use today to change people's lives. The heart of Christmas begins with understanding we are not alone. Compassion is such a holy element of the Christmas story that it breaks through all of the noise, busyness, and commercialism of the Advent season.

Even Christmas Movies Point Us Toward Compassion!

You know about my love for Christmas stories and movies, and I can tell you that at the center of almost all of them is a call back to the heart of Christmas. In *It's a Wonderful Life*, George Bailey finds out that it is his compassion as a businessman that makes him essential to so many families in the small town of Bedford Falls. In the famous Christmas stop-motion animated special, it is Rudolph's compassion for his friends Hermey the Elf, the misfit toys, and even the Abominable Snowman that brings them all back home with a role to play in saving Christmas. Come to think of it, even the movie *Frosty the Snowman* has a great moment of compassion when Frosty chooses to sacrifice himself in the greenhouse so his friend Karen can stay warm!

I don't know if there is a cultural Christmas story that calls us back to the heart of Christmas quite like Charles Dickens's *A Christmas Carol*. There are several movie versions of the story, but I like the one where British actor George C. Scott plays Ebenezer Scrooge—a man who loathes Christmas. In one important scene the main character responds harshly when asked to give money to the

COME HOME TO COMPASSION

poor: "I wish to be left alone," says Scrooge. "Since you ask me what I wish, gentlemen, that is my answer." When the men asking for donations press further, explaining to Scrooge that less fortunate people would rather die than have their families separated and sent to poor houses, he replies coldly, "If they would rather die, they had better do it, and decrease the surplus population."[7]

Of course, at the end of the story, Ebenezer Scrooge is completely transformed into a compassionate and warm-hearted person. In fact, he becomes famous for how he celebrates Christmas with his giving. The story challenges us to live like it is Christmas throughout the year. What I found interesting about this Christmas story is that the author, Charles Dickens, wrote out of very painful first-hand life experiences.

When Dickens was only twelve years old, he was forced to work ten-hour days in a rat-infested shoe polish factory because his father, mother, five brothers, and sisters (aged two to eleven) were put in prison over a family debt. It was compassion formed in real-life experiences that led to this famous Christmas story, and I can't help but wonder if that is why it had such a big impact on people. Charles Dickens's writing and activism on behalf of the poor made a big difference in Christmas giving, and he was instrumental in changing the lives of the less fortunate in England. People changed their behavior after they read his book; in fact, one wealthy businessman, after hearing the story read aloud by

Dickens in Boston on Christmas Eve in 1867, decided to close his factory for Christmas and bought all his workers a turkey to celebrate the day with their families, just like Scrooge did in the story. (Most people didn't get Christmas Day off work back in the late 1800s.[8]) Compassion leads to that kind of giving!

The First Christmas Gift

Of course, Christmas is a time for gift-giving. Maybe you've been out fighting the crowds at the store today, trying to make some progress on your Christmas list. There were presents at the very first Christmas, too, but they weren't left under a tree. They were carried by men who had traveled a great distance following a star to find baby Jesus. If you read about the history of Christmas celebrations, you'll find that the wise men's gifts to Jesus are a big part of why we have the tradition of giving gifts at Christmas today. Matthew wrote about the arrival of the wise men who were the first to bring gifts to the newborn Messiah: "When they saw the star, they were overjoyed. On coming to the house, they saw the child with his mother Mary, and they bowed down and worshiped him. Then they opened their treasures and presented him with gifts of gold, frankincense and myrrh" (Matthew 2:10–11).

I don't know about you, but I've always been interested

in why they brought these kinds of gifts for a child. As I've read more about it, I've found that the gifts likely held special spiritual significance. Even the popular Christmas carol "We Three Kings" reflects the belief that the gifts were meant to tell us something about Jesus Himself. The wise men's offering of gold represented His kingship. Frankincense was supposed to symbolize His priestly role. And finally, myrrh was a sign of Jesus' eventual death and embalming, His sacrifice for us, which is sung in the third verse of the carol, "Sorrowing, sighing, bleeding, dying, sealed in the stone-cold tomb." So, these Christmas gifts for the Messiah point to the significance of His sacrifice for us. The fact that baby Jesus received a gift signifying His journey to crucifixion is overwhelming to think about. Mary, Joseph, the shepherds, and the wise men were worshiping the newborn King, celebrating the birth of the Messiah, and yet He was given a gift that pointed toward the cross where He would one day give the ultimate gift, His life.

Christmas Is a Story of Compassion

We talk about events surrounding the first Christmas and the characters who arrived to worship Jesus, but how often do we consider the simple fact that Jesus, honored as a king and a priest by the wise men, was fully immersed in the human experience? Baby Jesus was helpless in that manger on that silent and holy night. Have you ever wondered why God didn't just send Jesus to earth fully grown? Why didn't He just descend from the clouds in a lightning bolt and start His ministry? Jesus, just like every one of us as infants, had to be swaddled, rocked, cradled, and fed by His mother. Jesus had to learn to crawl before He learned to walk. He cried when He was hungry. He had to learn to form His first words. Jesus had to learn to play as a child. He had to be schooled. And as He grew into boyhood, He learned a trade as a carpenter.

When I drive by the local live nativity scene at the church near my house and see Mary and Joseph, the angels, the wise men, the shepherds, and the animals, I don't usually think about the truth that my Savior was as helpless and innocent as we are at birth. Remember that compassion starts with simply understanding that you are not alone. And the humanness of Jesus proves God's deep love and compassion for us. Why? Because Christmas was the beginning of God's only Son walking a mile in our shoes! Jesus experienced nearly everything we experience: the joy and the grief, the laughter and the tears, the ups and the downs, the loneliness and the love. When we think about the baby lying in the manger, we should think of how much compassion Jesus would bring to the universe because He knows our emotions and our pain. Jesus was fully human, and He experienced the kinds of things that humans experience by virtue of being human.

Why is the idea that Jesus came close to us and experienced what it is to be human so vital to the truth of Christmas? Just think about how difficult it is to communicate with someone when you are far away from them. Distance can create a separation that is hard to overcome. Coming home for Christmas means being invited home by our heavenly Father. And so that first Christmas is simply God closing the distance by coming face-to-face with us in the person of Jesus, so there is no more separation between us. And God didn't just come closer; He experienced everything we can go through as human beings.

This brings me back to the very first Christmas gifts and the compassion of Jesus. The first Christmas gifts pointed the world to the ultimate Christmas gift born out of God's compassion for us. Did the wise men really understand how the Messiah would change the world with His death and resurrection? Were they anointing Him for the sacrifice He would make to cover the distance between you and me and our heavenly Father? Jesus experienced intense pain during His time here on earth—from weeping over the grief of His friends when Lazarus died, to sweating blood as He prayed in the garden for God to deliver Him from what was to come, to the gruesome realities He faced in His crucifixion, to ultimately suffering on the cross for our sins. The fact that He willingly went through this experience for us brings a powerful meaning to the name Immanuel—"God with us." He Himself is our gift.

COME HOME FOR CHRISTMAS

Snow-Shoveling Angels and Other Gifts

When I was a kid growing up in the Chicago suburbs, there was never a shortage of snow, which meant one of our weekly chores included shoveling the driveway at my childhood home. But my dad always took it a step further. Whenever a particularly heavy snowfall would hit, my dad knew there were several neighbors who would need assistance. The elderly widow down the block. The single mom on the next street over. The family from our church who had just lost a loved one. So, it was the "angels of the night" to the rescue! Picture a scene straight out of a Marvel superhero movie (except our only superpower was that we had shovels). My dad would take my brothers and me out late at night in secret to shovel the driveways and pour salt on the front steps of these homes. Neighbors would wake up the next morning and wonder who'd taken care of all the snow for them. The angels of the night had struck again!

One of the reasons I love the Christmas season is that even in the middle of all the terrible news headlines, great stories break through that inspire us to be better givers and better followers of Jesus. Compassion is always the catalyst for giving. I love when I hear stories of compassion, like the local restaurant owner who closed his doors to the public on Christmas Day and instead invited the homeless to come in for a free meal. What he began on his own at his little restaurant as a small act of kindness grew into a yearly collaboration with multiple restaurants and local volunteers who serve food and distribute warm clothing to those in need.

I am inspired by the story of a local church that learned about a struggling single mother who was unable to afford Christmas presents for her children and was about to be evicted from her apartment. The church community rallied together, collecting gifts and groceries, and even anonymously paid the landlord for six months of rent so this single mom could get back on her feet. In late November 2020, just before the Advent season began, a large church in Cincinnati partnered with a nonprofit and, in one weekend of services, raised enough money to pay off forty-six million dollars in medical debt for nearly forty-five thousand families.[9]

I'd be lying if I said I was always a willing participant in the winter good-deed gang. Spending hours in the bitter cold shoveling someone else's snow wasn't the average teenager's idea of a good time. I preferred sledding on snow rather than removing it from driveways and sidewalks. But my dad always made this a fun adventure, filled with thermoses of hot chocolate and plenty of snowball fights with each other. And in the end, it felt good to know that a neighbor in need would wake up to a pleasant surprise.

What if we all chose to be angels of the night at Christmas? We don't have to look far to find someone who could be greatly blessed by an act of compassion or kindness. And I love that my dad taught us the value of doing good in secret, not seeking glory or credit. There was a great feeling of fulfillment just knowing we were able to be givers of compassion to someone in need. Coming home to Christmas means coming home to the story of a Savior who has walked in our shoes and wants to help. To follow Jesus means that we accept His invitation to share in His compassion for the world.

Compassion Is the Heart of the Savior

We talk about Christmas gifts and Christmas as the season of giving, but the reality is, as Christ followers, it isn't just about giving—it is about honoring Christ's gift to us by being sacrificial in the way we give to others. Jesus is clear when He calls us to take up our cross and follow Him (Matthew 16:24). We are to love people the way God loves us and give to others in the same way God has given to us—a sacrificial way. And that means we have to embrace the heart of compassion. The New Testament understanding of the word *compassion* is best described as a gut-level intense emotion that moves people to relieve the suffering of others—to act. Jesus was pretty straightforward that compassionate living is *how* we love our neighbors. He preached about compassion throughout His ministry. We see compassion practiced both in His actions and in the way He taught His disciples to live.

When a group of religious leaders called Pharisees questioned Jesus about why He would hang around folks who weren't in the religious in-crowd, He quoted the Hebrew scripture to set them straight: "Go and learn what this means: 'I desire mercy [*compassion*], not sacrifice.' For I have not come to call the righteous, but sinners" (Matthew 9:10–13). In most translations of the New Testament, the words *mercy* and *compassion* are interchangeable. Later, when Jesus had just finished preaching to a large congregation for several days, He told His disciples He was concerned about their well-being: "Jesus called His disciples to Him and said, 'I feel compassion for the people, because they have remained with Me now for three days and have nothing to eat; and I do not want to send them away hungry, for they might faint on the way'" (Matthew 15:32 NASB). Of course, we know how that story ends. Jesus fed the large group of four thousand men with only seven loaves and a few fish. His compassion led to miracles.

COMPASSION DRAWS US CLOSER

Jesus always pointed out to His followers how differently the kingdom of God works. In a world that is all about getting, Jesus explained how we will be held accountable for our giving. He said, "Give, and it will be given to you. A good measure, pressed down, shaken together and running over, will be poured into your lap. For with the measure you use, it will be measured to you" (Luke 6:38). This verse has often been misused to imply that by giving you can get rich. But Jesus was saying the more you give, the more you engage in a compassionate way of life, the closer you are to Him, the more fulfilling your life becomes! You can't give sacrificially like Jesus and not experience Him. This isn't rocket science. It is always more fulfilling to give than to receive—that is the good news of the kingdom of God.

WE HAVE TO PASS IT ON!

As Christians, we believe in God's ultimate act of compassion—gifting the world with Jesus. If we have experienced the grace and forgiveness of Jesus while we were still sinners, how can we not be compassionate to others? Remember that coming home for Christmas means we are invited home to the Father's loving embrace. If we don't see ourselves as one forgiven and invited home in grace, we cannot have the compassion necessary to love others the way Christ calls us to. Because we are invited home for Christmas with open arms, we are supposed to invite others home!

So many of the most compassionate and giving people I've met are the same ones who have experienced remarkable difficulties, come through huge challenges, or experienced great forgiveness. And so, as we come to Christmas, it is helpful to ask the questions: What part of your story does God want to take and turn into compassion for others? How can God's redemptive work in your life help you understand someone else's pain and help them through it? Remember, the heart of Christmas begins with the gift of God making clear to us that we are not alone in anything we experience in life!

Right in the middle of the pain, God can turn your struggle into a deep level of compassion to reach out and heal others in need. Maybe the very people who need you most this Christmas are the ones to whom you can say, "I've been there too." I can tell you about my friend Sean, who lost his wife and now leads a grief recovery group for those who have lost their spouses. Or Jason, who is a recovered drug addict and now volunteers as a counselor at a faith-based rehab center. Cedric was once homeless and jobless and now helps run a shelter that provides clothes for interviews and job training for those in need. Joe is a veteran who came home from war with PTSD and now helps other vets deal with the lasting effects of their time in combat. And there is Jan, who nearly lost her marriage and now counsels young couples on how to maintain a strong relationship. These people are compassionate kingdom builders because they have truly walked in the shoes of the people they minister to. Their stories challenge us to live like it is Christmas throughout the year!

COMPASSION GOES BEYOND CHRISTMAS

I still think about Dax whenever I see Christmas decorations out at the stores in October. Sadly, he lost his battle with acute myeloid leukemia on Wednesday, December 30, 2009—just two short days before the New Year. But growing out of that terrible season of grief and pain, the Dax Locke Foundation was created by his mother, Julie Locke Moore. When the foundation began, they set a goal of raising $1.6 million to run St. Jude Children's Research Hospital for one whole day, and they hit it by organizing fundraisers and through all the connections in the community that were formed during the early Christmas celebrations.

Today the organization serves hundreds of families each year through a range of activities and initiatives. The Dax Locke Foundation now funds the operating costs of Camp Hope, which hosts more than 150 campers annually at no cost. It is a week-long summer camp that allows children who have been diagnosed with cancer or other blood disorders to safely participate in a variety of activities while being monitored by medical professionals. Julie helped spearhead efforts to bring a Ronald McDonald House to Peoria, Illinois, and continues to organize fundraising events. She oversees the Dax Locke Foundation's support for the Peoria Ronald McDonald House, which has pledged to build a "Dax Wing" for children with compromised immune systems. The wing is lined with "First Responders Hero Rooms," uniquely designed to encourage and uplift families whose children are experiencing medical difficulties.[10]

Dax's story, the way it brought people together, and the way it sparked an outbreak of compassion was so powerful that it was made into a movie. The film was meant to honor Dax's life story and to inspire others to give their time, efforts, and presence to others in the same way. The producer of the movie asked me to write a song called "The Heart of Christmas," which we took to the town of Washington, Illinois, and played at an event to raise money for St. Jude. Julie went through some difficult times in the years after Dax went home to Jesus, but I will never forget when she came up to talk with me at one of my shows years later to tell me that she had accepted Jesus into her heart! Even in the most tragic of circumstances, Julie witnessed Immanuel ("God with us") through the actions of the community, and now God uses Julie to do the same thing for countless hundreds of families each year facing difficult circumstances. I am always amazed by the way God works. What began with the compassionate response of a community grew into a beautiful story that invites us all home to the heart of Christmas.

It makes me want to give more. Growing up, I noticed that my dad was always giving his time, his presence, and even his resources to help people in need. Christmas Day was usually a day set aside for family. The church work was done, and the priority was for the West house to spend time together, from opening presents to hosting aunts, uncles, cousins, and grandparents. But we also knew that no matter what day it was, Dad was never off duty when it came to looking after people in our church or our community. Christmas Day for Dad too often meant visits to the hospital or to the homes of families in crisis. I learned that we had a mission as a family to give and serve and be compassionate to others—even when it seemed inconvenient. Here's the thing: compassion can often seem "inconvenient" in the moment.

Over the years, I have realized the moments when I have the opportunity to give to people are so much more meaningful than any career milestone, number one song, or any other kind of personal achievement. It is the moments of getting to lead worship in a prison, deliver supplies to those in need on a mission trip, or just sit and pray with someone who is going through a tough time that actually bring me into closer proximity to Jesus. Because any time we take a step into compassionate action, we will find Jesus right there at work. And those are the eternal moments that matter. I guess Dad showed us that being compassionate like Jesus means that as we show up for others, we are showing others the way home too. I believe coming home for Christmas means coming home to the greatest gift of Jesus. It means letting our gratitude for the compassion of a Savior and Friend who willingly walked a mile in our shoes move us to model that compassion to a lost and hurting world around us.

COME HOME QUESTIONS

+ Why do you think God sent Jesus into the world as a helpless baby instead of a conquering king?

+ How have you experienced compassion from others, and how did it point you to Jesus?

+ What healing experiences or lessons in your life can you use to share God's love with others?

+ How can you give to others in a sacrificial way this season?

+ Christmas is the story of God showing compassion for you. How can you show others that same compassion this Christmas season?

Seven

COME HOME TO FORGIVENESS

When God Runs Out to Meet You

I GUESS THIS IS THE CHAPTER FOR SOME IMPORtant Christmastime confessions. This time of year usually involves a lot of conversations with your kids about Santa Claus and his off-season activity of making a list and checking it twice. It is a great way to keep everyone on their best behavior in the weeks leading up to Christmas. (Because no kid has ever cared about what Santa thinks in July.) I don't know if you remember the scene at the beginning of *Elf* when the "big guy" informs Buddy that his birth dad (Walter Hobbs) is on the naughty list. The camera cuts to this gigantic book on a table with pages and pages of names while Buddy screams a long, drawn-out "Noooooo!!!" as if it is the worst news he could ever imagine hearing.

Christmas lore tells us Santa puts lumps of coal in naughty kids' stockings. I never got coal for Christmas and have never met anyone who did, although we might have deserved it. One year, my church put on a Christmas play called "The Sixth Grade Scrooge." I had the lead role and played a disobedient sixth grader who broke his foot after riding his bicycle when he wasn't supposed to. You could say I was born to play that role. I know you're going to be really surprised to hear this, but I wasn't always a perfect kid. When I think back to Christmases past, I'm not proud of some of my behavior. I guess I'll confess and let the court of public opinion decide.

For starters, when we were young, my brothers and I would get up *really* early before the sun was up on Christmas morning every year. The three of us began a tradition of making our parents breakfast in bed. But we weren't competing to be the best children in the world; there were completely selfish motives going on. We learned that the smell of bacon and a freshly brewed pot of coffee was also a great way to get Mom and Dad out of bed and the Christmas festivities started. It always proceeded to be the messiest and worst breakfast ever. The bacon was burned. So was the toast. The eggs were runny, and the coffee was weak. The goal was not to delight our parents with a culinary masterpiece. We selfishly just wanted to get them out of bed so we could get to opening those presents under the tree. I'll always remember the looks on Mom's and Dad's faces as they politely pretended to enjoy their terrible breakfast.

And speaking of those presents under the tree . . . I'll leave you with one more Christmas confession. The West boys devised an elaborate plan one year to sneak a peek at our Christmas presents before Christmas Day. There weren't many places to hide gifts in that little three-bedroom, one-bath house. So, we knew where Mom was stashing our presents. Our curiosity got the best of us, and we ruined the beautiful surprise of Christmas morning because we just had to sneak into the attic and check out our gifts early. I remember feeling so guilty on Christmas morning as I pretended to be surprised by each and every gift, and I wished I hadn't been so selfish. (Mom, if you're reading this, I'm sorry!)

The idea of Santa Claus keeping a list and checking it twice is funny, but sadly, it is often the way we live our lives and think about God. Sure, we can joke about the idea of the big guy in the red suit up in the North Pole writing down everything we do and keeping a list of the good and bad, but that is the exact opposite of how the Bible tells us we should live. When it comes to keeping score of my own mess-ups, I'm usually the first one to take note. I'll beat myself up for something I said in a heated work conversation (even after I apologize). I'll get busy and miss my morning prayer time. Sometimes I'll get impatient and snap at the girls in the middle of our morning routine to get out the door. The point is that I am almost a professional bookkeeper when it comes to keeping track of my own wrongdoings. I don't even need Santa to make a list and check it twice because I am doing that work for him. But the more we track our own naughty list, the more we find ourselves paying attention to the wrongs of others. The older I get, the more I understand that keeping a list like that breaks God's heart.

If you are reading this and you are married, you know that you can't be a scorekeeper and be in a loving and healthy relationship. Sometimes, when my wife and I get into a fight, and I know she is mad at me, I'll come up to her acting really earnest, and I'll try to make it sound like I am going to apologize. "I have something I want to say to you . . . (I'll grab her attention with a long, sincere pause.) I forgive you." It usually gets her to laugh and breaks the ice for me to really apologize, but we have learned together that keeping a record of our mess-ups only gets in the way of the two of us being close.

The exact same thing happens in my walk with God. Those moments when I beat myself up because I am keeping score spiritually are the very times when I lose the theme of the story—that He is always inviting me home into His presence. He is always saying, "I forgive you." The Bible clearly teaches in 1 Corinthians 13:5 that love "keeps no record of wrongs." So why do we spend so much time being so hard on ourselves?

Making a List and Checking It Twice

Embracing forgiveness starts with just letting go of your list—the one where you try to pretend to be perfect and hold others to the same standard. Maybe you can relate, but I have this terrible habit of wanting *everything* to be just right at Christmas. I love the holidays so much that I build up a picture of what Christmas should look like and how it should all unfold. Year after year, I find that I am just setting myself up for constant disappointment. Why? Because we live in an imperfect world with imperfect people! Plans have to change because of work deadlines or someone gets sick. Flights get delayed because of weather. Dinner gets overcooked sometimes. Even the most perfectly thought-out presents end up being returned for one reason or another. The Christmas perfectionist in me always reminds me of Clark Griswold in *Christmas Vacation*. I can so easily relate to his fatal flaw of wanting the perfect holiday—just like his failed attempts to put up the Christmas lights on the outside of his house. I feel like Clark sometimes when he has a total meltdown in front of the entire family because the highly anticipated (and needed) Christmas bonus was swapped out by his boss for a lousy jelly-of-the-month-club membership. I always laugh out loud when his wife says, "It's just that I know how you build things up in your mind, Sparky . . ."[11]

I'm learning how much those built-up idyllic visions of how I believe my holidays should look and feel can actually get in the way of me being able to enjoy Christmas. So many of us try to hold ourselves and others to an unreasonable standard of perfection and mark ourselves down on the list as a failure when things (inevitably) end up being imperfect. The problem with that way of living is that when we keep a list about ourselves or others, we also are rejecting God's gift of forgiveness. We put ourselves above Him as judge and jury by acting like we can be disqualified from His grace. When we don't embrace the truth that we are made perfectly imperfect—all of us—it keeps us far from home and far from the heart of Christmas. Maybe we just need to be reminded that even the first Christmas is a story of God using imperfect people in imperfect circumstances to bring perfect forgiveness into the world.

Even Christmas Is an Imperfect Story

No one could read about the very first Christmas and think that it happened perfectly. Remember that the innkeeper, or whoever they were staying with in Bethlehem, turned Mary and Joseph away because there was no room for them.

After all that travel (ninety miles or so), they had to shack up with a bunch of animals and use a manger as a crib for the divine baby! And what about the wise men who went to see King Herod at his palace when they were looking for Jesus? Not such a wise move. But they still somehow made their way to worship the newborn Messiah. And the shepherds? They sure weren't in a perfect position to come into town looking for Jesus. They were in the middle of a shift at work when the sky lit up with heavenly hosts telling them to go find and worship the newborn Messiah. The people weren't perfect, and the circumstances were far from it. But we celebrate Christmas because a perfect love entered into a far-from-perfect world that night.

The reason Jesus was born, as the angel Gabriel told Mary in the Gospel of Matthew, was because He would "save his people from their sins" (1:21). Jesus arrived into our world in the midst of our imperfection with forgiveness. Christmas is a time of coming home to forgiveness, and that begins with letting go of our ideas about perfection—in ourselves and in others. The great purpose of what was taking place around that little manger in the country town of Bethlehem was summarized by the apostle Paul in Romans: "But God showed his great love for us by sending Christ to die for us *while we were still sinners*" (5:8 NLT, emphasis added). It is the truth of Christmas that while we were missing the mark, while we were getting it wrong, while we did not deserve it or have a right to expect it—Jesus loved us so much that He moved into the neighborhood to be with us. The story of that holy night is that God sought a relationship with us even in the midst of all our imperfections.

Into the Father's Open Arms

If I had to leave my family with just one Bible story that reflects what is most important to know about God, it is the parable of the prodigal son. I can read it over and over and still be in awe of how much more I have yet to understand about the depth of God's love and forgiveness for me. In a world where we approach Him like He is a great scorekeeper in the sky, where we struggle to embrace forgiveness for ourselves and to offer it to others, we can always use a reminder of what Jesus taught us about what it means to come home. Jesus, the most engaging storyteller ever, told His followers about a young man who would definitely be on the "naughty list." Jesus explained that this prodigal son asked his dad to have all his inheritance money and ran off to another country and spent every last dime on really poor life choices. Now, to get the full picture of what this young man did, you should know that in the first century if a son asked his father for inheritance money, it was the equivalent of wishing his father was dead. So the very act of asking for the money was not just insulting but also should've been relationship-ending.

COME HOME TO FORGIVENESS

The prodigal son found himself completely broke and living in terrible circumstances. He decided that even the lowest servants under his father's care were treated better: "'I will arise and go to my father, and I will say to him, "Father, I have sinned against heaven and before you. I am no longer worthy to be called your son. Treat me as one of your hired servants."' And he arose and came to his father" (Luke 15:18–20 ESV).

This prodigal son had insulted his father and spent all the money. After his actions, it seemed like it might be a perilous homecoming. I wonder if those listening to Jesus tell the story in real time thought that maybe the father would turn his son away. Maybe the son would have to repay the money he took before being welcomed back into the family. Maybe he would just live with the servants and do manual labor the rest of his days. But Jesus' parable took an unexpected turn. "While he was still a long way off, his father saw him and felt compassion, and ran and embraced him and kissed him" (v. 20 ESV). In the first century, it would be considered humiliating for the head of a household to run anywhere. Only workers and servants ran to do anything. Yet, Jesus explained that when the dad saw his son, he didn't just walk to greet him—he ran to embrace him!

I think the son responded a lot like you or I would when his dad ran to him with open arms: "Father, I have sinned against heaven and before you. I am no longer worthy to be called your son" (v. 21 ESV). Jesus said that the father was so overjoyed that he didn't even acknowledge his son's confessions or groveling: "But the father said to his servants, 'Bring quickly the best robe, and put it on him, and put a ring on his hand, and shoes on his feet. And bring the fattened calf and kill it, and let us eat and celebrate. For this my son was dead, and is alive again; he was lost, and is found.' And they began to celebrate" (vv. 22–24 ESV).

How many times have you felt lost and then found? How many times have you turned your face toward Jesus and found Him waiting there with open arms? This parable is about how our heavenly Father feels when we simply turn our hearts toward home. His forgiveness is a gift. There is no divine scorecard being kept. There isn't a naughty list to be settled. We don't have to live outside His house until we work off our debt. We don't have to be perfect. You see, the miles and miles of "I am not worthy, and I am not good enough" that may be separating you from coming home don't tell the true story. Jesus says we just have to turn our hearts toward Him, and He will dress us in honor and throw a party in our name.

The great problem with all our scorekeeping, perfectionism, and naughty lists is how they highlight the truth that we struggle to embrace God's love without conditions. And until we accept the gift of His grace and forgiveness in our life, we will not be able to love other people without conditions. Forgiveness is God's everlasting gift to us at Christmas. And as we receive that gift, He requires us to pass on the gift of forgiveness to others.

The Gift of Forgiveness

Jesus' followers apparently had a problem with forgiveness, in the same way you and I might. On one occasion, Peter asked Jesus if he was required to forgive someone as many as seven times. I don't know about you, but forgiving someone seven times seems like a lot. Jesus replied to Peter, "Not seven times, but seventy-seven times" (Matthew 18:22). Jesus was essentially saying that we are required to offer forgiveness to others as many times as it takes. We should forgive other people without limit because that is how God forgives us! So, in the kingdom of God, there is no naughty list that we can check twice.

Jesus spent a lot of time teaching about forgiveness throughout His ministry. Forgiveness is even central to the prayer that Jesus taught us all to pray, the Lord's Prayer, which includes: "Forgive us our sins, as we forgive those who sin against us" (Luke 11:4 NLT). Like so many things in church and religious culture, we sometimes recite this prayer without fully paying attention to the real meaning of its words. But Jesus, as He shows us how to pray, is pointing out that the forgiveness we receive from God is deeply connected to our willingness to forgive others. In another passage, Jesus made this even clearer: "If you forgive other people when they sin against you, your heavenly Father will also forgive you" (Matthew 6:14). Not only is the gift of forgiveness one that we receive from God, but it is also a gift we are required to freely give away.

THE DISTANCE TO FORGIVENESS

When we talk about coming home for Christmas, the wonderful reality is that "covering the distance home" is simply understanding that the distance was covered for us—that while we were still sinners Christ died for us. The message of the gospel is the message of God running to us. So whenever and wherever we celebrate Christmas, we are celebrating the beginning of God's pursuit of us! Maybe it is important for some of you reading this right now to be reminded that if you just choose with all your heart to come home to forgiveness this Christmas, you'll find that the distance home isn't miles and miles; you can cover it by simply turning back toward Him. What a gift it is this Christmas to know that just like the prodigal son, while we were still a long way off—our heavenly Father came running to meet us (you and me) in the form of a baby wrapped in cloths and lying in a manger on that holy night in Bethlehem. Christmas was truly the night that perfect love and perfect forgiveness entered our imperfect and unforgiving world and changed it forever.

So, what does it look like for us to come home to

forgiveness this Christmas season? Well, it begins with us. What unforgiveness are you carrying in your heart today? What is keeping you from turning your face toward the One who offers forgiveness to you freely? I find that most of the people who are carrying the burden of not being able to forgive others are also the most unforgiving toward themselves. I have friends who talk like they are scared to darken the door of a church because of the list of wrong-doings they hold tightly. I know someone who jokingly said that there was too much distance between him and God because of the things he had done in his life. He said, "I don't really think praying will help me, because I am not sure God would even recognize the sound of my voice." That is a lot for a person to carry, but my friend is missing out on what Jesus says about the character of God. The Father never forgets the sound of His child's voice and is always ready, waiting, and willing to run toward us with open arms. Forgiveness is a free gift that is always just one ask away.

Aside from naughty lists and coal in stockings, the Christmas holidays are when we come face-to-face with some of the most painful conflicts in our lives that have gone unresolved throughout the year. It is the season when we feel the weight of strained or broken relationships. I think this happens because Christmastime makes us dream of what our world would look like if it were set right. The holidays bring us face-to-face with the need for healing and forgiveness in our lives and in our community. It isn't always easy to deal with these things.

I know someone whose father attempted to reconnect with him after years and years of estrangement. They had a long history of conflicts, and it was difficult for them to even carry on a phone conversation. Then there are the two childhood friends who haven't spoken in decades because of differing political views. Another Christmas will pass without them talking to each other. A neighborhood friend tearfully explained to me how stressful her family Christmas dinner gathering would be this year because it is the time that her brothers and sisters choose to air out all their problems and vent their frustrations with one another. I have another friend who will have to go visit his younger brother in prison this Christmas season because the rest of the family refuses to forgive him for his mistakes. These situations are tough. They require the same humility and bravery that the prodigal had to muster to return to a father he had disrespected. But, like the star in the eastern sky guided the shepherds, somehow Christmas points us in the direction of home—to forgiveness.

FORGIVENESS IS THE WAY BACK HOME

Here is a truth about Christmas that extends to the rest of your life. Without receiving and offering forgiveness, you cannot experience all that it means to come home for

Christmas. When you carry the burden of the weight of your naughty list, there can be no joy. When you drag the heavy chains of your unforgiveness toward others, you cannot experience the peace that passes all understanding. It is difficult to embrace the wonder of Christmas without first accepting the free gift of God's forgiveness. Do you want to truly live with a free and compassionate heart? Do you want to be able to give freely? And what about healing? Well, throughout the New Testament, Jesus forgave as He healed. We know from Scripture that all you have to do is repent, meaning to turn your life toward your true home in Jesus, and you will be welcomed into His house (1 John 1:9). The way back home isn't super complicated; it starts with accepting God's gift of forgiveness.

I've often told the story about that amazing day on the blue couch in the basement of my family's home in Downers Grove, Illinois. I came home from school that afternoon hoping to watch my Chicago Cubs play, but I turned on the television to find Billy Graham preaching. That was the day that I accepted Jesus into my heart. And that was the day I asked to be forgiven of my sins. After that television sermon, I turned my heart back toward my Father's house. And ever since then I have been learning how to live a life of forgiveness. I recently found an article that the Reverend Graham wrote about the meaning of Christmas. I can still hear his voice as I read these words that remind me of how important it is for us to let go of our efforts to be perfect, our long list of wrongs, and our grudges toward others, and simply come home to His forgiveness:

> The Christmas message says that God's grace is greater than our sin. It says that the sin question was answered at the cross. Christmas says that the cross went as deep as our needs. The cross was the cure—offered, paid for and administered by a loving God in His beloved Son.[12]

One of the reasons that we need Christmas more than ever is because the world needs forgiveness and forgiven people who will forgive others—more than it ever has. So maybe it's time we stop living like God keeps a big, long book on an official table with pages and pages of names and a list of all our wrongdoings. The Bible tells us our sins have been removed from us "as far as the east is from the west" (Psalm 103:12). I don't know how far that is exactly, but it seems an immeasurable distance. Maybe it is time to turn back to the Father's house and accept the forgiveness He is offering you. Maybe it is time to start living like a person who has received God's grace and been welcomed home. As you're making your Christmas list this year, could it be the perfect season to begin making a list of the people that you need to forgive even more than seventy-seven times?

I think we should try to make Christmastime the "resolution for forgiveness" season! Let's not wrap another gift or eat another cookie without first celebrating Jesus' birth by forgiving others. Christmas is the season that invites restoration into the world, and it can begin with you right now in this very moment. Ask God to help you truly receive His forgiveness so you can forgive—knowing the distance between you and forgiveness has already been traveled by a Savior. From the perfection of heaven, Jesus carried a perfect love to an imperfect world. And with a simple act of forgiveness, you can participate in His work to bring the world back to Him.

Is there someone in your family you need to forgive or ask for forgiveness? Someone in your office? A friend? Maybe it is finally time for you to tear up that list you are keeping in your mind and simply forgive yourself. I want to invite you to follow the way home toward Christmas this season and offer forgiveness to those who have hurt and disappointed you in the past. Imagine a Christmas when your heart is completely overcome with joy, peace, wonder, compassion, and healing. The Father is waiting for you to come home to forgiveness this Christmas.

COME HOME QUESTIONS

- What are some ideas of perfection in your life that get in the way of receiving or offering forgiveness?

- Do you have a funny story about being on the naughty list as a kid?

- Do you have a list of things for which you have been unwilling to accept God's forgiveness?

- Is there someone who comes to mind today whom God wants you to forgive?

- How can asking for, accepting, or offering forgiveness help you experience peace and joy this Christmas?

- What does the story of the prodigal son say about God's invitation for you to come home to Him?

Eight

COME HOME TO THE MANGER

The Most Cherished Gift

EACH CHRISTMAS WHEN I WAS A KID, LIKE CLOCK-work, and no matter what was going on, I could always count on receiving a blunt, circular object wrapped in plain green and red tissue paper. It was as dependable as the Christmas tree going up on Thanksgiving weekend and Santa's visit always happening *after* I finally fell asleep. I just knew it would always be there. Now, I've always been that guy who inspects presents carefully when no one is watching. So, if the size, shape, and wrapping paper didn't give it away, the fact that its contents always jingled when I picked it up and shook it confirmed what was inside the carefully wrapped gift. As I got older, I didn't even bother checking it before I opened it. You see, every single year of my childhood, this was the little package left for me at Christmas from my grandma Luella West.

Now, let me remind you that Grandma raised ten kids, and most of them got married and had kids of their own. So she literally had a small village of grandchildren to buy for at Christmas. My grandparents never had much money anyway, but after my grandpa passed away in 1984, things were even tighter for my grandma. No matter the circumstances of her life, she always welcomed a visit from all the members of the big West clan. And she enjoyed celebrating during our annual Christmas visits to northern Iowa, even later in her life when she was dealing with health issues. My grandma never let her situation stop her from giving a Christmas gift to each of her many grandchildren. There was something special about the simplicity and sacrifice in her giving that still sticks with me all these years later.

I guess I understand very clearly now how hard she had to work and how carefully she had to save throughout the year just so I could hold that blunt, jingling object in my hands each Christmas. I remember those moments when my brother and I would sit together and unwrap Grandma's gift to find the same Gerber baby food jar. That was her offering to us each year. A container, carefully wrapped and filled with one hundred pennies. Each and every one of the West grandchildren received a dollar for Christmas.

Of course, as a kid, you are always going to be more allured by the bigger gifts like a pair of Nikes, baseball cards, or a remote-controlled car. Those were the kinds of things we received from our parents and other relatives on Christmas morning. As the presents were opened, I would politely thank my grandma for her gift and then quickly set it aside (secretly disappointed), ready to move on to the more flashy and exciting ones. I'll admit, at the time, the significance of her gift was lost on me. The sacrifice Grandma West made to give us that dollar went completely unappreciated. To be honest, most years I held out hope that she would give me something different. But there it was, year after year after year, a blunt, round, jingly baby food jar filled with a hundred pennies.

As I grew older and wiser, I began to realize what it meant for her to give all of us that gift. It actually became a cherished moment that I always looked forward to at Christmas. My brother and I began to anticipate her present with some teenage humor like, "Where are you going to spend your dollar from Grandma?" But in reality, we had grown to really treasure her intention.

I don't know if I fully understood how much my grandma's faithful giving truly captured the heart of Christmas until the year I graduated from college. I remember that she was one of my biggest cheerleaders and was always so proud of me. She was also really supportive of my music dreams and let everyone know about it. When you are just starting out, faith and belief from the people who love you can be like wind in your sails. I always laugh when I think about how she used to tell me that I was going to be the next Elvis Presley! And I will never forget our visit when she sat me down and told me, "Matthew, someday you're going to play the Grand Ole Opry!" You know, she wound up being right (about the Grand Ole Opry, not Elvis). She had really big hopes for me. The Christmas before I graduated from college, she presented me with another blunt, jingly gift wrapped in the same paper as every year, but this one was somewhat bigger than what I had come to expect in years past. That particular present would be the best Christmas gift I ever received. You know, when I think back on my life now, the memories of all the big, flashy, or expensive Christmas presents I got as a kid have faded away, but I still remember Grandma West's. And I am still impacted by the lesson her gift taught me about the heart of Christmas.

Coming Home to the Gift

We have talked about all the things at Christmas that can distract us from its true meaning. As you know by now, Christmas is my absolute favorite holiday, but I am aware it is all too often commercial, material, full of big price tags, big events, big noise, and constant busyness. Even in the

West house, sometimes we go big with our celebrations and stack the presents taller than the one who is opening them! Many of us can take the holiday celebrations a little bit over the top. But if I'm being honest, while all those things are fun, they aren't ever the truly meaningful moments. None of them make Christmas the homecoming it is supposed to be. I still think often about Grandma West and how the simplicity and sacrifice of her giving continually points me toward the heart of that first Christmas and the manger. Because the true story of Christmas is the gift of a humble King in humble beginnings. When we take a break from the chaos of the season and stop looking to fill the empty spaces in our lives with the world's empty promises and false hopes, we find the meaning, intention, and sacrifice all right there in God's love story to us.

As we come to the end of this book, I want to invite you to turn your heart back toward the greatest gift ever given. This Christmas I have challenged you to say yes to God's invitation home and offer that invitation to those who need a home. I have dared you to embrace the wonder, joy, healing, compassion, and forgiveness that the Christ child brings this season. But most importantly, I want you to remember this Christmas how all God's blessings began, with the unexpected gift of eternal hope lying in a manger two thousand years ago in Bethlehem. I want you to take time this Christmas to bring your attention to the moment the Savior arrived. In a world that says go big or go home,

God entered creation in the most unassuming town, in the most understated circumstance, in a most unassertive form.

Searching in the Nativity

As we sing lines like "The hopes and fears of all the years are met in thee tonight" each Christmas, it reminds me of the longing in the hearts of all those characters in the story of Jesus' birth. The nativity scene is filled with people who were searching, much like we are today. Mary and Joseph had been searching for a place to stay because there was no room in the inn. The wise men traveled hundreds of miles looking for a Messiah at the end of that star and searching for the truth of what His arrival could mean to the world. The shepherds in their fields at night came into that little town searching to find the truth about what the angels had proclaimed. And the Prince of Peace arrived at that moment of history, not in a palace in the capital city but in a barn. He was laid in a manger and surrounded by animals. The simplicity of Jesus' birth is such a stark alternative to how our world celebrates it today, but the longing for hope was the same.

All those characters who were searching for something arrived to worship Jesus at the manger. All of them were caught up in that holy moment. Matthew tells us about how the wise men worshiped Him: "On coming to the house, they saw the child with his mother Mary, and they bowed down and worshiped him" (2:11). They were deeply moved by being in the presence of the Prince of Peace. Luke explains that the shepherds were too: "When they had seen him, they spread the word concerning what had been told them about this child" (2:17). And even Mary, who had waited in hope for her first child to be born, was caught up in the otherworldly significance of this sacred moment: "But Mary treasured up all these things and pondered them in her heart" (Luke 2:19). All these characters came to the first Christmas like you and I do: longing for something bigger than us, searching for something unchangeable, needing something we can lean on in the chaos and uncertainty of the world. The searching and longing of every human heart in history could end that holy night because the hope of the world had finally arrived.

I'm amazed that ever since that first Christmas in Bethlehem, we still come to the celebration of Jesus' birth longing for the same thing when He is right there waiting for us with outstretched arms. *Hope.* Still, we grasp for temporary fixes and chase after the allure of the world's false hopes. As followers of Jesus, I think we too often get distracted by these lesser hopes. All the cultural Christmas stories I have written about in this book reflect a common longing for hope to arrive at Christmastime. In *A Christmas Carol*, Scrooge's nephew stops by each year, holding out hope that Ebenezer will join him for Christmas dinner.

Rudolph hopes Santa will find a way to accept him. Buddy the Elf hopes for a reunion with his real dad. And everyone at the North Pole hopes that a single dad named Scott Calvin will accept his new role as Santa's replacement and save Christmas in *The Santa Clause*. But there is no more powerful Christmas illustration of our hopelessness than the plight of my guy George Bailey and his crisis that leads him to the brink of suicide. These stories resonate because they reflect a truth about humanity and the real longing we carry with us into every Christmas season.

Hope Is Calling at Christmas

I love reading the story of what happened between the warring armies during World War I around Christmas. German and British soldiers were huddled in their trenches on Christmas Eve, trying to celebrate the holiday as best they could in the middle of a brutal and hopeless situation. But it was Christmas. Even in the midst of war, something simple and unexpected took place. All along the front lines, soldiers on both sides began to leave their trenches without weapons and met enemy soldiers in the middle! They ate, drank, shared cigarettes, sang Christmas carols, and played games together. What happened was so amazing that it is still written about in history books.[13] These men, who were under orders to kill each other, began celebrating the holidays together as if they were long-lost friends. The Christmas celebrations broke out all over the front lines of the war, even though the commanders of both armies weren't happy about it. I love this story because it reflects the truth of what has been happening at Christmas ever since that first night in Bethlehem: hope comes calling for us. I believe we have a longing for hope embedded in our DNA as human beings—if only we would look to the One who is our gift of hope.

So, what exactly is this gift of hope we are talking about at Christmas? It isn't something we want or something we wish for; the hope we celebrate as Christians is grounded in a holy confidence. We can live in expectation because our hope is found in the person of the resurrected Jesus. Hebrews reminds us what it means to have Jesus as our hope: "We have this hope as an anchor for the soul, firm and secure" (6:19). Jesus, the greatest gift, is the very thing that anchors us—He is the Source of our hope. And the Prince of Peace isn't just the Source; He is also the One who provides us with that hope. The apostle Peter explained a little more about what that hope means: "Praise be to the God and Father of our Lord Jesus Christ! In his great mercy he has given us new birth into a living hope through the resurrection of Jesus Christ from the dead" (1 Peter 1:3). Hope is only found in Him, and every time we look around for hope in other places, whenever we get caught up with the big, flashy, hollow promises of the world, we will come up empty. We can embrace hope not in some far-off time but in the here and now because the greatest gift of all arrived on that first Christmas. Hope arrived. Hope was delivered. Jesus came as a man, He lived, He died, He was crucified, and He rose again, and that very hope is calling to us today.

This gift of hope at Christmas isn't a naive one. It isn't a hope that sticks its head in the sand and ignores the chaos of the world. The hope found in Jesus doesn't deny how broken things really are in the world around us. In fact, I don't know if we can really embrace true eternal hope without acknowledging the pain of sin in our lives, in our neighborhood, and in the world at large. But our hope looks at all that is wrong in the world and knows confidently that it will be fixed one day when Christ returns. There is more to the story. This most unexpected gift of Christmas, which arrived to us in the humble beginnings of a manger, has rewritten all of history by conquering sin and death.

This is what it truly means to come home for Christmas, to accept the invitation to receive God's greatest gift of eternal hope. We are anchored in the love of our God, who is the same yesterday, today, tomorrow, and forever (Hebrews 13:8). The gift of hope fixes our gaze on Jesus instead of our circumstances. Because there is Christmas, we can have hope in a God who is not moved, no matter our situation. We can maintain that hope in God because

His character is the same no matter what conditions we face. Jesus is the one steady and consistent gift in a world that is unreliable, untrustworthy, and ever-changing. And why is this gift so unexpected? Because He is faithful, even when we are faithless. And when our eyes are fixed on the One born in a manger, we can offer that simple gift of unexpected and eternal hope to the world around us.

Be the Bearers of Hope

I've told you a little bit about life as a preacher's kid. Christmas for my friends' families was a time when most parents were able to clock out of work for a few days or so, but I learned that the job of a preacher is never done—especially during the holidays. What I witnessed growing up in the house of a pastor was that so many people reached the end of their hope at Christmastime. We didn't have cell phones back then. You could actually take your phone off the hook if you didn't care to be bothered. (I know this is all very twentieth-century information—but if you tried to call, you would get a busy signal!) I can still remember how many people would call the landline at our house to talk to Dad when they needed hope. I learned that our longing for real hope doesn't take a day off just because it is Christmas. In fact, during the holidays those feelings are often elevated to levels that are unbearable for many a human heart.

Dad never really clocked out during the holidays, and I always knew that he was going to have to run out on Christmas to help someone. However, I learned an important lesson about our responsibility as followers of Jesus while growing up in the West house: If we have the hope of Jesus, we have an obligation to bring that message of hope wherever and whenever there is hopelessness. I have tried to carry that with me into my own ministry work.

Every Christmas, one of the functions of our ministry, called Popwe, is to step into stories and let people know that no matter what is going on in their lives, there is always hope. Each year we try to remind people of this in practical ways. We will often pinpoint families who are going through a tough time at Christmas and surprise them with a financial gift as a way of sharing the hope of Jesus. Recently we found a family in Kansas who had experienced a really bad car accident that had left their son severely injured. We were able to jump on a Zoom call and surprise them with a gift to help them through that Christmas season. I'll never forget the spirit of that young man on the call as he was making jokes and laughing with me, even in the midst of his difficult season of recovery. He explained that his favorite song of mine was called "Mended," where I sing a verse about the truth that where we see ourselves as "wounded," God already sees us as "mended." I got off that call that day and was reminded that we serve a God who always sees the other side of what we may feel is hopeless. I was trying to spread the hope of Jesus, and I received that hope right back tenfold!

The Simple, Sacrificial, Unexpected Gift of Hope

The most important message I want to leave you with this Christmas is that the hope found in Jesus is truly the ultimate gift. Why? Because our resurrected Savior has the final say in our story. And whenever I think of the greatest gift, it takes me back to the simplicity, sacrifice, love, and meaning of those yearly offerings from my Grandma West. I still can get emotional about the Christmas I visited Grandma as I was getting ready to graduate from college. I remember holding that heavier, well-wrapped, jingly package in my hand as a young man, more aware than ever before of the sacrifice that yearly gift required of her. I think it was the first time a Christmas gift really moved me to the point of tears. As I sat there that day talking with my grandma at our annual West family Christmas visit, I carefully unwrapped her gift to find it was not the same one hundred pennies I had grown accustomed to receiving for the last twenty-four years of my life. I had to fight back my emotions as I looked into the clear jar. It still jingled and rattled like all the others, but this year she had filled the large glass container not with pennies but with thirty silver dollars. It was an *extravagant* gift for her to give. When I looked up at Grandma, she seemed so much older than all the years of my childhood. I gave her a hug and thanked her and, at that moment, the real significance of her faithful presents throughout my life really hit me. Grandma West's simple, sacrificial, unexpected offering of thirty silver dollars is, to this very day, the most meaningful Christmas gift I've ever received.

I guess that moment with my grandma reminds me of what Christmas is truly about. A God who gives sacrificially and extravagantly. It reminds me of my heavenly Father, whose simple and unexpected gift of hope is my anchor. I really believe that Christmas calls us home. I think that is why I love this season so much. That is why I started to invite everyone to Franklin, Tennessee, to experience the West family Christmas with me each year. Because coming home means coming back to the real significance and meaning of that nativity scene in the Gospels. You know, in the same way that my Grandma West's final gift to me became the most authentic, memorable, and unexpected Christmas gift of my young life, the gift of hope in Jesus shines through the darkness, flooding out the allure of all the world's false hopes.

When we come home to the greatest gift of all, we are coming home to eternal hope.

We are coming home to the Son of God, the Prince of Peace, who has reigned with His Father since the beginning of time. The Bible tells us that our hope has been present since the foundation of the world. As the Gospel of John explains: "In the beginning was the Word, and the Word was with God, and the Word was God. He was with God in the beginning. Through him all things were made; without him nothing was made that has been made" (1:1–3). At Christmastime, we celebrate the moment the eternal Creator entered into His creation for the sake of hope. The Creator who spoke the heavens into existence, who breathed life into man, was laid down as a helpless child in a manger on that holy night in Bethlehem to offer us hope. Jesus took on human limitations and began His journey to the cross with our hope in mind. He is the greatest gift we could ever receive; He is just as the Gospel of John describes Him: "The light shines in the darkness, and the darkness has not overcome it" (John 1:5).

I want to invite you to bring all that seems hopeless in your life right now to Jesus. I hope you will come and kneel before Him at the manger this season. When you choose to come home for Christmas, there is no financial crisis, there is no diagnosis, there is no addiction, there is no broken relationship, there is no pain, there is nothing that can overcome the hope of Christ. There is no darkness His light can't shine through. You can lean on the unexpected hope found in Jesus. It is the greatest Christmas present you could ever receive.

There is a gift waiting for you this season, and I

promise it has been there each and every Christmas of your life, calling you to turn around and come home. Wherever you are today, it is past time to say yes to the invitation home for the holidays. Maybe it is time to open your eyes to the wonder of God's entrance into the world on that night in Bethlehem. What if you allowed the joy and peace of the Savior to invade every part of your life? What would it look like this Christmas to embrace the healing and forgiveness that is available to everyone who calls on His name? You know, underneath all the decorations, fancy presents, laughter, and stress of these holiday gatherings, there is the truth of that scene around the manger. There is the holy night and the simple story of an unexpected gift. The longing of your heart for hope this Christmas is pointing you back to the most important moment in the history of the world. And that beautiful gift born in Bethlehem is alive today and calling you to come home for Christmas . . . to come home to Him . . . to come home for good.

COME HOME QUESTIONS

- What is the most meaningful Christmas gift you have ever received? Why?

- In which areas of your life are you struggling with hope?

- How does your heart long to come home for Christmas this season?

- How is the gift of hope found in the person of Jesus different from the hope the world offers?

- What does the word *hope* mean to you? What are you hoping for this Christmas season?

COME HOME TO THE PROMISE

An Empty Seat at the Table

I DON'T THINK I COULD FINISH A BOOK ABOUT COM-
ing home for Christmas without addressing the grief so many
of us carry, especially during this time of year. After all, the
real "afterword" to all of our stories, the last sentence, the
final say, is caught up in the great promise of Christmas.
Every Christmas, my family takes time to remember the
loved ones we've lost by keeping an empty seat at the table
that reminds us of the ones we miss. My dad's brother Jim
lost his life serving our country during the Vietnam War.
So even in the joy and chaos of those huge family gatherings each Christmas, there was always an underlying sadness

about who was not with us. I remember how Grandma West was quietly missing Grandpa in the years following his passing. And now my family takes time to remember Grandma West, who has gone home to be with Jesus. (I named my daughter Lulu after her, so I often think of Grandma when I say her name.) We all will have an empty seat or two at the table at Christmas, and I know so many of you may be too familiar with the ache of missing someone this season. But it is also true that without the grief, loss, chaos, unrest, sin, and death in our world, there would be no reason for Christmas.

For so many of us, Christmas is a reminder that there is brokenness in this world that only heaven will set right. When I think of the empty chair around Grandma West's table, it reminds me of a song I wrote with my friend Mark Hall from Casting Crowns, called "Scars in Heaven." The song's lyrics capture the reality that even in our grief, we can come home to the promise that this life on earth is not the end of the story. Healing is promised because heaven awaits. Because of Bethlehem, we have a Savior who has overcome death. The Gospel of John shares Jesus' promise to us about eternity: "I go and prepare a *place* for you" (14:3, emphasis added). And even as He hung on the cross, in the midst of excruciating suffering, Jesus told one of the criminals next to Him, "Truly I tell you, today you will be with me in paradise" (Luke 23:43). The manger leads to a cross, which leads to an empty tomb, and just as angels announced good news, an angel would affirm God's promise in the Gospel of Luke: "Why do you look for the living among the dead? He is not here; he has risen!" (24:5–6).

Jesus' words are the final truth of Christmas, the great afterword of God's love story—that all of those who have accepted Him will come home to the glory and the promise of heaven. The Messiah, who was worshiped by shepherds and wise men, was lying in a manger and was the great Light breaking through the darkness. Because of that holy night in Bethlehem, we can hold fast to the truth that the last chapter of our story is coming home into the arms of our heavenly Father. Because of the promise of heaven, our tears of grief will turn to tears of joy, and our deepest questions will be answered. Because of heaven, the empty chairs at the table will lead to beautiful reunions. Because of the promise of Christmas, none of our goodbyes are final.

It is my prayer that you will be comforted by the reality that because of Christmas, the grief of separation from those we've lost is only temporary in the light of eternity. This season I want to invite you to come home to the promise of heaven and look forward to the joy-filled reunifications in our final homecoming.

Because a manger led to a cross and a cross led to an empty tomb.

Because Jesus is preparing a place for you and for me, where all of our empty chairs around the table will be filled once again when, because of Christmas, we can finally come home to heaven.

WEST FAMILY
CHRISTMAS RECIPES

World's Best Brussel Sprouts

3 tablespoons butter
1 small onion, chopped
2-3 pounds Brussels sprouts, washed, drained,
  and cut in half
Salt and pepper to taste
$1/2$ teaspoon cayenne pepper
$1/2$ teaspoon paprika
1 $1/2$ cups heavy cream
$1/2$ cup shredded sharp white Cheddar cheese
$1/2$ cup gruyere cheese

Preheat oven to 375 degrees. In a large skillet over
medium heat cook bacon until crispy; drain and set aside.

Add onion and Brussels sprouts to bacon drippings. Add salt, pepper, cayenne, and paprika. Cook for 10 minutes. Add cream, cheeses, and bacon. Bake for 12-15 minutes.

Sweet Potato Casserole

1 cup sugar
1/2 cup evaporated milk
Pinch of salt
2 eggs
1 teaspoon vanilla
1/3 cup butter

In a large bowl, add the sweet potatoes, sugar, milk, salt, eggs, vanilla, and butter and mix well. Pour into a 9x13-inch baking dish.

Topping:
1 cup brown sugar
1 cup coconut
1/3 cup melted butter

Combine flour, brown sugar, coconut, and butter in a bowl and sprinkle over sweet potato mixture. Cook at 350 degrees for 35-40 minutes.

Corn Casserole

1 can corn kernels
2 eggs (slightly beaten)
1 package corn bread mix (I use Jiffy)
1 stick melted butter

In a large bowl, combine the corns, eggs, corn bread mix, and butter and mix well. Place in a lightly greased 8x8 pan. Bake for 45 minutes at 350 degrees.

Apple Pecan Corn Bread Dressing

4 cups herb-seasoned dry bread stuffing mix
2 tablespoons chopped parsley
$1/2$ teaspoon ginger
$1/2$ teaspoon salt
$3/4$ cup butter
1 cup chopped celery
2 cups apple juice
2 cups chopped apples
3 eggs
$1/2$ cup chopped pecans

Preheat oven to 350 degrees. In a large bowl combine and corn bread, stuffing, parsley, ginger, and salt. In a heavy saucepan, melt the butter and sauté the celery for 8-10 minutes or until tender. Add this mixture to the cornbread mixture and mix well. Stir in the apple juice, chopped apples, eggs, and pecans. Spoon into greased casserole dish. Cook for 30-35 minutes.

Monkey Bread

2 teaspoons cinnamon
3 (12 ounce) packages of refrigerated biscuit dough
$^1/_2$ cup butter
1 cup brown sugar
$^1/_2$ cup chopped nuts (but you can leave these out if you prefer)

Preheat the oven to 350 degrees. Mix the granulated sugar and cinnamon in a large ziplock bag. Cut each biscuit into four pieces. Drop the biscuit dough in the bag of cinnamon-sugar mixture to coat the pieces. Place each piece into a well-greased bundt pan (I coat a few at a time then drop them in). Once all of the biscuit dough is in the pan, melt the butter and brown sugar in a small pan over high heat on the stovetop. Once sugar has dissolved, pour it over the biscuits. Bake for 35 minutes. Remove from oven and place the pan on the counter for 5 minutes, then flip it over onto a plate. Serve warm and gooey.

Chess Pie

2 cups white sugar
1 teaspoon vanilla
4 eggs
1 tablespoon cornmeal
1/4 cup evaporated milk
1 tablespoon distilled white vinegar
1 unbaked 9-inch pie crust

Preheat the oven to 475 degrees. In a large bowl, mix the butter, sugar, and vanilla together. Mix in the eggs. Then stir in the cornmeal, evaporated milk, and vinegar until smooth. Bake for 10 minutes in the pre-heated oven, then reduce the heat to 300 degrees for 40 minutes. Let cool. Top with whipped cream.

ACKNOWLEDGMENTS

THIS BOOK ABOUT COMING HOME FOR CHRISTMAS was able to be brought home and across the finish line thanks to the efforts of an incredible team I'm blessed to have surrounding me.

Matt Litton—I'm thankful for our writing partnership. Your gifts are on full display once again on these pages.

Kyle Olund, Brooke Miller, Katherine Hudencial, Elizabeth Hawkins, and the entire team at W Publishing— Thank you for your belief in me and the ideas I'm always dreaming up!

Steve Green—Your wisdom and navigation throughout the publishing process is always spot-on and much appreciated.

Story House Collective—Thank you for helping me manage a crazy schedule so that this book could be created!

My family—Your love and support mean the world to me. Love you!

NOTES

1. C. S. Lewis, *Surprised by Joy: The Shape of My Early Life* (San Diego: Harcourt, Inc., 1955), 18.

2. Bible Apps, s.v. "joy (*n.*)," accessed April 8, 2024, https://bibleapps.com/j/joy.htm.

3. "Isaiah," Biography, Hearst Digital Media, updated August 13, 2019, https://www.biography.com/religious-figures/isaiah.

4. Jessica Booth, "Anxiety Statistics and Facts," *Forbes Health*, updated October 23, 2023, https://www.forbes.com/health/mind/anxiety-statistics/.

5. *Christmas Vacation*, directed by Jeremiah Chechik (1989; Burbank, CA: Warner Home Video, 2008), DVD.

6. Jill Jackson and Sy Miller, "History of Hymns: 'Let There Be Peace on Earth,'" Discipleship Ministries, June 12, 2013, https://www.umcdiscipleship.org/resources/history-of-hymns-let-there-be-peace-on-earth.

7. Charles Dickens, *A Christmas Carol* (London, 1843; Project Gutenberg, updated March 2018), https://www.gutenberg.org/files/46/46-h/46-h.htm.

8. Sara Kettler, "Charles Dickens Wrote 'A Christmas Carol' in Only Six Weeks," Biography, updated December 15, 2020, https://www.biography.com/authors-writers /charles-dickens-a-christmas-carol.

9. Madeline Mitchell, "Crossroads Church Leverages Donations to Wipe Out $46.5 Million in Medical Debt," *Cincinnati Enquirer*, updated March 7, 2020, https://www.cincinnati.com/story/news/2020/02/24 /crossroads-church-nonprofit-wipe-out-46-5-million -medical-debt/4854753002/.

10. Julie Locke Moore: "The Dax Foundation," *Peoria*, November 2019, https://ww2.peoriamagazines.com /pm/2019/nov/julie-locke-moore.

11. *Christmas Vacation*.

12. Billy Graham, "Billy Graham's Message: Christmas, a Time of Renewed Hope," Billy Graham Evangelistic Association of Canada, (1969) December 14, 2022, https://www.billygraham.ca/stories/billy-grahams -message-christmas-a-time-of-renewed-hope/.

13. A. J. Baime and Volker Janssen, "WWI's Christmas Truce: When Fighting Paused for the Holiday," History, updated February 26, 2024, https://www.history.com /news/christmas-truce-1914-world-war-i-soldier-accounts.

ABOUT THE AUTHOR

MATTHEW WEST HAS BUILT HIS CAREER AS A revered storyteller. The five-time Grammy® nominee, dubbed by *Billboard* as "one of Christian music's most prolific singer-songwriters," has been awarded multiple RIAA Gold and Platinum certifications, notched thirty number-one songs combined as an artist and songwriter, and has more than 250 songwriting credits to his name.

Matthew is passionate about providing hope and healing through the power of song, prayer, and story. *Come Home for Christmas* marks his eighth book, following *My Story, Your Glory: A 30-Day Devotional*; *Give This Christmas Away*; *The Story Of Your Life*; *Forgiveness*; *Today Is Day One*; *Hello, My Name Is*; and *The God Who Stays*. The new thirty-day devotional was inspired by his 22-track album of the same title that was released in 2023.

Matthew and his wife, Emily, live in Nashville with their two daughters, Lulu and Delaney.

About the Writer

Matt Litton is a bestselling writer with three #1 *Publishers Weekly* and *Wall Street Journal* nonfiction bestselling books. His recent projects include *My Story, Your Glory: A 30-Day Devotional* by Matthew West (with Matt Litton), *On Our Knees* by Phil Wickham (with Matt Litton), and *In the Presence of Jesus* by Paul Bane & Matt Litton. Matt resides in Nashville with his wife and family. You can read more about Matt and his work at www.mattlitton.com.